Christianity--Is It Really True?

Responsible Faith In A Post-Christian Culture

Ron Highfield

ISBN: 1515344681
ISBN 13: 9781515344681

I wish to express my heartfelt gratitude to Niels C. Nielsen, Jr., my dissertation advisor, mentor, advocate and friend. I will never forget the day in a seminar on Christology when the discussion turned to the resurrection of Jesus Christ. Some students believed in the bodily resurrection and some thought the resurrection to be at best a metaphor. Professor Nielsen listened patiently. When he finally spoke he said something to this effect, "By the resurrection, I mean that on Sunday morning after his death on Friday he was up walking around." I wanted to yell, "Halleluiah!" I thought it fitting to dedicate to him a book that focuses so much on the resurrection of Jesus. Thank you for that moment and every other way you have blessed my life!

CONTENTS

PREFACE

This book is second in a series of books I've written in weekly installments on my blog ifaqtheology (Infrequently Asked Questions in Theology). It contains in revised form the 48 essays I wrote between August 2014 and July 2015 on the question, "Is Christianity True?" I hope that publishing them in printed form will make them accessible to individuals and groups that want to study the topics of Christian evidences and Christian apologetics. I have long felt that the most popular works on evidences and apologetics don't quite get it right. As a whole they try to prove too much and do not take adequately into account our fallibility. They underestimate the role of the will in belief. And they too readily accept the burden of proof, which puts the case for Christianity at a decisive disadvantage. They do not take the best logical and rhetorical path from nonbelief to full Christian faith. Specifically and most disturbingly, they attempt to prove the Bible's authority independently of faith in the resurrection of Jesus Christ from the dead. In this book I develop a different understanding of the path to faith, a different vision of the role of the will in belief and a different way of establishing the authority of the Bible.

Part One sets out the ground rules for Christian evidences. The chapters in this section will clarify the purpose, methods and limits of evidences. We will ask who bears the burden of proof and what conditions must be present before an inquirer can make a reasonable judgment to believe the Christian gospel and a responsible decision to take up the Christian way of life. We define such relevant terms as truth, reality, certainty, knowledge, faith and opinion. Finally, we will map the path from nonbelief through four decision points to full Christian faith.

Part Two takes us through the four decision points we must traverse on our way to full Christian faith. First, we must decide between atheism and belief in God. I argue that this decision depends on our choice between matter and mind as the most fundamental explanation for our world. Is the beginning and end of all things spirit or matter, life or death, intelligible or unintelligible, mind or machine? Having decided that believing in God is the most rational choice, we now confront the second decision point where we ask, "Is the mind that is evident in the intelligible order of the world impersonal or personal?" If we opt for a personal God, a third decision point confronts us with the choice between thinking of God as the highest aspect of nature or as transcendent over nature. Is God supernatural or natural? Is the world God's creation or God's body? The issue can also be framed as a decision between theism and panentheism, which is the idea that God is an aspect of the world neither wholly different from world nor fully identical to it. If we accept theism as the best answer to this third question, we come to the fourth decision point at which we must decide whether to remain mere theists or move into full Christian faith. At this crossroads we are required to discuss the possibility and actuality of a revelation of God in history. At the moment of decision we must assess the evidence for the bodily resurrection of Jesus Christ from the dead and reflect on the meaning of this event for the nature, identity and significance of Jesus.

Part Three marks the transition into a new phase of the argument for Christianity's truth. The previous chapters presented an affirmative case for making a reasonable judgment for Christianity's truth and a responsible decision to become a Christian. But now we must deal with some misunderstandings and objections to Christianity. The positive side of the argument is often called "Christian Evidences" and the defensive side is often called "Christian Apologetics" or "Defense of Christianity." The necessity of the defensive phase of the argument rests first on the propensity of people to misunderstand what Christianity actually is and what it really teaches. How can we make a reasonable judgment or a responsible decision about Christianity unless we possess an accurate understanding of its teachings? Some people find certain versions of Christianity incredible or morally offensive or insufferably superficial, and hence hesitate to accept them. Others adopt a form of Christianity that is defective when compared to the original form taught by Jesus and the apostles. It is questionable whether one has really made an authentic decision about Christianity if the form they know is not the real thing.

The second reason for the pursuing the defensive phase of the argument arises from the barrage of objections that nonbelievers hurl against Christianity. Some raise objections to the existence of God, theism or divine revelation. They raise the problem of evil or assert that the world needs no explanation beyond itself. Others object to the moral teachings of the Bible or deny its historical accuracy. Some offer objections to the reliability of the apostolic witnesses to the resurrection of Jesus or object to the very possibility of miracles. The list is endless. And even if one thinks the case I made in the first phase of the argument is very strong, one may still be disturbed and caused to doubt by the many objections that are raised. Hence I want to reply to some of the most potent objections. Some of these objections may turn out to be based on misunderstandings of Christianity. But some may accurately represent Christianity and yet still suggest reasons to doubt or reject it.

How to Read This Book

I wrote this book as a sustained and step-by-step argument, and reading it from beginning to end may be the best way to get the most from it. But I think there are several points at which readers could enter the argument without getting lost. If you are not interested right away in the question of methods in apologetics, you could skip Part One and move directly to Part Two, which develops the four decision points on the way to full Christian faith. And even within Part Two, you could read the chapters on the fourth decision point, which focuses on the resurrection of Jesus Christ, without reading the first three. Or, you could begin with Part Three, which deals with objections to Christian faith. No matter where you begin, I hope you will read the whole book so that you can see the big picture argument.

Part One

THE RULES FOR CHRISTIAN EVIDENCES

Part One sets the ground rules for Christian evidences. In the following chapters I will clarify the purpose, methods and limits of evidences. We will ask who bears the burden of proof and what conditions must be present before an inquirer can make a reasonable judgment to believe the Christian gospel and a responsible decision to take up the Christian way of life. We will define such relevant terms as truth, reality, certainty, knowledge, faith and opinion. Finally, we will map the path from nonbelief through four decision points to full Christian faith.

1

UNDERSTANDING THE QUESTION

There are plenty of good books that present evidence for the truth of Christianity and defend it from attack. Why do we need another? Because there are also plenty of books that deny Christianity's truth and attack it in new ways and from almost every conceivable angle! Hence the work of Christian evidences and apologetics is never done. Christian truth does not change, but contemporary culture and thought change almost daily. To communicate effectively with our contemporaries we must listen to them, come to understand their most basic beliefs and values and learn how to explain Christian faith to them in ways they can understand. This task is not easy to accomplish, and there is no shortage of failed attempts. Indeed the Christian cause suffers almost as much from its friends as it does from its enemies. Many efforts to support and defend Christianity have done as much damage as good and created as much doubt as confidence in the Christian faith. Some arguments for Christianity overstate their case and understate the force of objections. Others try to prove too many things. Good thinkers from the time of Socrates until today know that making bad arguments in favor of a good cause is worse than silence.

In the course of this book I hope to clear away some bad arguments, confused language and rash and uninformed claims made by believers. And of course I will do the same with bad arguments made by nonbelievers. I will attempt never to misrepresent what we can know and what we cannot. I want to state fairly the case against belief as well as for it. I want to be clear about the kind of evidence I am presenting. Is it a claim to historical fact, a logical truth, a metaphysical truth, a practical truth, speculation, opinion, trust in the reliability of others or religious experience? I want to be clear about what I am asking the reader to do in response: to open their minds to alternative views, accept a conclusion as possible, preferable, probable or true. At minimum, I want to clarify the choices we must make and what is at stake in each.

I will not try to *prove* that God exists or that Christianity is true. Proof is a strong word. It applies only to a limited number of activities, mostly in logic and mathematics. And even proofs in these areas begin with unproven axioms. The "proved" conclusions in logic or mathematics are true only if the axioms are really true. Logic and mathematics use clear and simple language and don't challenge us morally, existentially or spiritually. Philosophical and theological approaches to religious questions deal with highly complex data and must use language that is far from clear and simple. And they deal with the most important, challenging and emotion-laden questions human beings ask.

What is at stake in the question, "Is Christianity true?" Exactly what is this question asking? (1) Am I asking about how we can *show* that Christianity is true? Perhaps you are a believer but you have limited ability to give reasons for your faith. Your inability may limit your capacity to engage with unbelievers on a rational level, and hopefully this book will improve your ability to explain and defend your faith. (2) Or, am I asking "Are you *certain* that it is true?" Certainty is a desirable state of mind because your level of certainty may affect your joy and your willingness to live thoroughly as a Christian. But the question of certainty is not the same as the question of truth. Certainty is a subjective measure. People have been completely certain of things that turned out to be false. And our lack of personal certainty is not good evidence for the falsity of what we believe.

(3) Or, am I asking about the difference for the meaning of human existence between the truth and the falsehood of Christianity's claims? Each of these interpretations is worth pursuing. But the third interpretation gets at the central issue I want to address. The claims of Christianity are either true or false. If they are false, every hope, moral rule, comfort and belief that depends exclusively on their truth is also false. Likewise, if the claims of Christianity are true, every hope, way of life and belief that depends on them is also true. If you think that nothing of existential or moral consequence depends on the truth of Christianity, then you won't be very interested in the question. It does not matter either way. But that view itself is contestable, and refuting it is a very important part of my argument.

The question, "Is Christianity true?" cannot be limited to the particular claims Christianity makes about Jesus of Nazareth. Certainly, if Jesus Christ is not the Son of God and Lord and did not rise from the dead, Christianity is false. But Christianity also makes claims about God and the world. If there is no God, Christianity cannot be true. If there are millions of gods, Christianity cannot be true. If God is not good, Christianity is false. If materialism is true, Christianity cannot be true. If the divine nature is completely unknowable, Christianity cannot be true. Hence in addressing the question about the truth of Christianity I plan on dealing with the most comprehensive issues involved in this question. Do we have reasons to think anything really exists other than matter? Does it make sense to believe in God? Where do we begin in moving from belief in God to full Christian faith?

In the next chapter we will begin to clarify some concepts needed to think about the truth of Christianity. I find that many people have no clear understanding of such concepts as reality, truth, falsehood, fact, knowledge, opinion, subjective, objective, history and many others. We will think first about the qualifiers *real* and *true.*

2

PURSUING A HUGE QUESTION

Is Christianity really true? Where shall we begin to answer such a huge question? Medieval theologians used to say, "Method does not matter." This saying makes sense when you consider that the English word "method" is derived ultimately from the Greek word *"methodos,"* which means "a following after" or "pursuit" or "access." Christianity is a complex belief system, and one can begin thinking about it at any point within it. What matters is not where you begin but that you "pursue" the whole system of faith to the end.

Different people find themselves at different points in the journey from nonbelief to faith. For some, their faith in God is unshakable but their belief in Jesus is tenuous. Others find Jesus' moral teaching compelling but the church's claims about him dubious. Still others find themselves at other places on the way from nonbelief to full faith. Ideally, this book would begin by addressing each person's most pressing question and move from there to cover the entire system of belief. Demanding that everyone begin their quest for deeper faith at the same point would be as foolish as demanding that everyone who wants to go to New York City must begin at Los Angeles. You begin where you are. Hence there are as many beginning places and ways of "pursuing" the question of Christianity's truth as there are individuals.

Obviously, I cannot begin with each reader's individual questions in a book written for whoever happens to read it. I must use another way, a more general method that will eventually cover all the questions in an orderly way. Two methods come to mind as possibilities. We could follow the "order of knowing" or the "order of being." If we followed the order of knowing, we would ask ourselves, "What are the first, second and third things one needs to know in order to make the journey from nonbelief to full faith?" Once we settle on an order of knowing, the outline of our argument follows easily. Though this method has its famous champions, I will not take this approach.

Following the order of being, we would ask ourselves, "What is the order of reality, in order of priority, presupposed and asserted by the Christian faith?" In other words, "What must be true about the way things really are, in order of priority, if Christianity really is true?" Do I begin with the issue of the origin of the world or the first cause of everything or the existence and nature of God? Or, is some other question the best candidate for first place in the order of being? I will follow this method in this book. Along the way, I will explain why I prefer it.

3

WHICH "CHRISTIANITY" IS TRUE?

It does little good to argue for Christianity's truth unless we are clear about what we mean by "Christianity." Impressions of Christianity are as numerous as observers, and many quite different systems of belief and practice present themselves as Christianity. Christianity has been identified with western culture, democracy and progressive morality. Some religious thinkers identify Christianity as a system of metaphysical beliefs, and others deny that Christianity asserts any metaphysical truths. It makes sense, then, to spend a little time pursuing the meaning of the term "Christianity." Even if complete unanimity of opinion is too unrealistic a goal to hope for, surely no one would argue that Christianity is whatever every Tom, Dick and Harry say it is.

Christianity can be defined descriptively or normatively. In a descriptive definition, Christianity is defined as the system of beliefs and practices cherished by people who self-identify as Christians. Descriptive students of Christianity use historical or social science methods of measurement. For Christians in the 5th century, for example, Christianity is the system believed and practiced by them. Christianity today is whatever contemporary self-identifying Christians believe and practice. Clearly, a purely descriptive method cannot supply a definition of Christianity suitable for the task of answering the question, "Is Christianity true?" If Christianity is whatever self-identifying Christians of any age believe and practice, there are many Christianities, not just one. Indeed, as defined descriptively, there are many Christianities in every age. And it makes no sense to ask which one is true. You can find the most astonishing diversity of belief and practice among self-identifying Christians and churches even in one city. Whose Christianity are we talking about?

Obviously, we also need a normative definition of Christianity. In a normative approach, a system of belief and practice must have certain essential elements to qualify as Christianity. Apart from these elements, a system is not Christianity at all. For normative thinkers, there is no such thing as atheistic Christianity or Christianity without Christ or Gnostic Christianity. Calling such systems of belief and practice "Christianity" is mistaken and misleading. Hence an apologetic argument for the truth of Christianity cannot avoid the perpetual debate among self-identified "Christians" about the essential elements of authentic Christianity. What sense does it make to argue that Christianity is true, if Christianity possess no essential, identifiable characteristics?

I will use both descriptive and normative approaches in this book. We need both. I will attempt to clarify the essential elements of Christianity and exclude some variants as impostures. For this chapter, however, let me define Christianity descriptively, in very general and preliminary way. *Christianity is a distinct system of religious and moral beliefs and practices that points to a transcendent divine reality that acts for the salvation of the world from evil and the fulfillment of creation's potential.* For the present, let's leave aside the task of enumerating and clarifying those beliefs and practices and focus on this formal definition.

Christianity is more than "a distinct system of religious beliefs and practices," but it is at least that. It is an interlocking system of beliefs and practices that embody these beliefs in specific actions. If Christianity were just a practical way of life or merely a set of religious feelings, the question of its truth would be out of place. The question, "Is Christianity true?" makes sense only if the essential nature of Christianity can be identified and Christianity makes specific claims about reality that can be assessed for their truth value. The project of answering the question "Is Christianity true?" will need to clarify what those claims are and examine the evidence for their truth.

4

WHAT IS "TRUTH" ANYWAY?

In March 1970, Jane Fonda appeared on the Dick Cavett Show. During the show, she had an interchange with the Archbishop of Canterbury, Michael Ramsey. "Jesus is the Son of God, you know," asserted the Archbishop. Fonda retorted, "Maybe he is for you, but he's not for me." The Archbishop of Canterbury replied dryly, "Well, either he is or he isn't." Fonda's view of truth demonstrates why we need to think about truth itself before we can make sense of the question, "Is Christianity True?"

"What is Truth?" It's difficult to say what Pilate meant when he asked Jesus this question (John 18:38). Jesus had just said that he came into the world "to bear witness to the truth" (18:37). Was Pilate skeptical of all truth claims or merely doubtful of Jesus' particular truth claims? When we hear the question, "What is truth?" we prepare ourselves for a deep discussion conducted in an obscure philosophical vocabulary. We have a feeling that we may be embarking on an interminable journey that ends right were we began, none the wiser for our trouble. In my view, that feeling of futility says something important I want to explore.

The question, "What is truth?" calls on us to think critically about a concept we use daily without difficulty, and this request may be the source of our sense of futility. We are being asked to explain something that seemed obvious before the question was asked. The concept of truth is so basic to our thought that we can't find terms more primitive with which to explain it. All language presupposes the concept of truth, even the language we use to define the concept of truth. At the end of a discussion about truth we could still ask, "Is our definition of truth true?" The discussion, then, begins again at the beginning!

Adjectives and Nouns

As interesting as I find philosophical discussions of the nature of truth, I want to begin by asserting that we already know what truth is. The meaning of truth is implicit in our everyday language. Let's begin with the simple distinction between the noun "truth" and the adjective "true." We learned in grammar school that a noun names a thing and an adjective modifies a noun. An adjective "modifies" a noun in that it names a particular property of the thing the noun names. As an example, consider the noun/adjective combination "navy blue slacks." The adjective "navy blue" names a property of the noun "slacks." Slacks can exist in different "modes" (brown, blue, gray, etc.) and the adjective specifies the particular "mode" in which these slacks exist. Hence the term "modify" is used of the function of adjectives.

We use the adjective "true" to modify sentences that assert facts. Such sentences are called "propositions." Only propositions can be true or false. Questions, exclamations, lone words and fragments cannot be true or false, because they do not make assertions. To put it in concrete terms, the sentence "God raised Jesus Christ from the dead" makes an assertion of fact. This sentence is either true or false. The adjective "true" modifies the assertion the sentence makes. As we pursue the question about Christianity's truth, we must ask about the truth of a set of propositions that make up Christianity's truth claims.

Truth and Reality

Let's think about the noun "truth." As I pointed out above, nouns name things. What does the noun "truth" name? It names a property of a proposition. Propositions can be true or false. A true proposition possesses the property "truth." Hence "truth" is a property that can be present or absent in propositions. But what is this property? What is its character, considered as a thing named by a noun?

To answer this question adequately I need to introduce another term, "reality" (or the thing itself). Implicit in language is a distinction between sentences and the things about which sentences speak. We know the difference between the sentence, "My coffee cup now sets on my desk, about one foot to my right and about an arm's length away," and the actual state of affairs described by the sentence. As I write, I am experiencing the actual state of affairs empirically, and the above sentence expresses my sense experience. You are experiencing the image the sentence puts into your mind, not the sense experience I am having. The sentence is a proposition and the real things (the desk, the distances, and the cup) are what the proposition refers to. It would make no sense to ask, "Are the real things true?" Truth is a property of propositions, not of things. Reality takes priority over truth, because propositions depend on reality for their truth. In my view, reality is an even more basic concept than truth. How do you define reality? I may try to say something about this later, but I will let it be for now.

So, what is truth? Truth is the property that exists in a proposition when that proposition corresponds adequately to reality, to the things it describes. Truth is not a synonym for reality, though it is often misused in this way. Truth is a relationship of correspondence between a proposition and reality.

Why is this discussion about the concepts of truth and reality important in our quest to answer the question, "Is Christianity true?" It is important because misuse of these concepts is very common in religious or moral discussions. We've all heard such statements as the following: "Truth is what is true for you." "Truth is what works for you." "Christianity is true for me." "All religions are true." Thoughtlessly accepting these statements deflates our passion for God and excuses our indifference and worldliness. I believe these thoughts on truth and reality demonstrate that statements like those above are not only thoughtless and mistaken but are downright nonsensical.

In this book, I will be asking whether the assertions Christianity makes about reality actually correspond to the reality about which it speaks. I can accept no other meaning to the question, "Is Christianity true?"

5

WHO BEARS THE BURDEN OF PROOF?

In the discussion between believers and nonbelievers, who bears the burden of proof? Who must present evidence, and who gets to decide whether the evidence is persuasive? The conventional wisdom is that the person affirming a belief must present evidence sufficient to move the one who doubts toward belief. Doubters do not need to make arguments for their doubt. And the doubter decides the question. Clearly, this presumption gives the doubter an almost insurmountable advantage in discussions with believers. Does the believer really bear the burden of proof?

Are propositions that affirm something inherently less likely to be true than propositions that deny something? Apart from knowing what is being affirmed and denied in the real world by these propositions, I can't see any reason for preferring one over the other. But what about real world affirmations and denials? Is there something inherent in the real world that makes doubt always the more rational option than belief? The answer is no. Everyone would agree that someone faced with overwhelming evidence in favor of an affirmation would be acting less rationally to deny that belief than to affirm it. For example, suppose I deny that my child smokes marijuana even when confronted with a video of my child actually smoking marijuana. Clearly, I would not be acting rationally in my denial. I am allowing wishes and prejudices rather than reason to determine my beliefs. Hence whether one believes or doubts is determined by more than the evidence presented on behalf of belief. It is also determined by one's beliefs about other things, by one's prejudices and values. In other words, the amount of evidence required to persuade people is determined by the entire situation in which the argument takes place.

Consider the rhetorical rules in a court of law. In a criminal case, the prosecution always bears the greater burden of proof and must convince 12 people "beyond a reasonable doubt" of the defendant's guilt. The defense need only create reasonable doubt in the minds of jurors. Why place this heavy burden on those affirming the proposition, "Defendant X murdered victim Y." Are defendants always more likely to be innocent than guilty? No, that is not the reason for the burden. The reason is that our legal system presupposes that it is morally superior and socially more expedient to let a guilty person go free than to convict an innocent one. So, the side that must bear the greater burden of proof in a court of law is determined by the special situation that applies in that setting.

Someone may make the following objection to what I have said so far: to move from not believing to believing a proposition (for example, God exists.) requires evidence, but doubting or denying a proposition requires no evidence. But this is not true. You need a reason to doubt an affirmation. After all, doubting is an action. We are compelled to doubt an affirmation when it conflicts with other beliefs, values, wishes or prejudices we possess. If you doubt or deny that God exists, you do so because you sense the conflict between the proposition "God exists" and other beliefs and values you hold. You may doubt God because you believe that "the physical world is all there is" or that "human freedom is not compatible with God's existence." But this means that the rationality of your doubt of God depends on the truth of your other beliefs and values, which themselves must be supported by evidence. The doubter gets no exemption from the need for evidence. Every argument between a believer and a nonbeliever always involves confrontation between two systems of mutually supporting beliefs. Both parties affirm and both deny certain beliefs. There is no such thing as pure doubt. To claim that one merely doubts is to deploy a rhetorical trick. Believers should be on guard against it.

I conclude that in the discussion about the truth of Christianity there are no general rules for who bears the greater burden of proof. There are no general rules for how much evidence is enough or what type of evidence counts in favor of Christian belief. And there is no objective third party qualified to declare when the burden has been met. The rhetorical situation in which the discussion takes place determines all these issues. Different people demand different levels and types of evidence and are moved by different arguments. In a particular phase of the discussion believers may need to present evidence for belief, but in a different phase nonbelievers will need to present evidence for their supporting beliefs, the beliefs that compel them to doubt.

It's as true in the argument between belief and nonbelief as it is in the economic sphere: there is no free lunch. There is not even a subsidized lunch.

6

CHRISTIAN BELIEF: KNOWLEDGE, FAITH, OPINION OR JUST WISHFUL THINKING?

In this chapter we will continue clarifying the basic vocabulary, framework and rules for the discussion. Many discussions about God's existence and Christianity's truth suffer from confusion. We get in a hurry, talk past one another and express our feelings rather than take the time to communicate clearly and understand each other. So, I believe it is necessary to give some time to these introductory matters.

In the previous chapters I've addressed the issues of truth and reality and the issue of who bears the burden of truth. In this chapter I will focus on knowledge. What does it mean to know something? In transitioning from truth to knowledge, we shift from the issue of the properties of propositions to the issue of how a proposition is held by a knower. In addressing the question "Is Christianity True?" how would it profit us to clarify what it means *to claim* that Christianity is true, if we have no idea what it would mean *to know* that Christianity is true? And, of course, in due time we need to secure that knowledge.

What is Knowledge?

What does it mean to know something? To say that we know something speaks about way a truth is held by the knower. First, knowledge concerns truth. Belief in a falsehood is not knowledge, no matter how certain you are of its truth and no matter how diligently you work to discover and test its truth. There is no such thing as mistaken knowledge. Second, believing a truth is not sufficient for knowledge. You may guess correctly how many fingers I am extending behind my back; that is not knowledge. Guessing, tossing the dice, accidents, wishful thinking and prejudices of all kinds, even if they hit on the truth do not count as knowledge. You need something else. The "something else" concerns the way you hold that truth to be true.

Contemporary philosophers differ on the exact thing needed to transform true beliefs into knowledge. We need either "justification" or "warrant" in addition to true belief. The justification criterion demands that we make a good faith effort to examine a belief and that we are able to give good reasons for accepting it as true. The warrant criterion focuses on the proper functioning of our belief-forming mechanisms. If our belief is true and it is formed under the right conditions and our belief-forming mechanisms are functioning properly, we possess knowledge. I am not going to take sides in this debate.

Does knowledge come in different quantities and qualities? The answer is yes. There is a qualitative scale of knowledge, with perfect or absolute knowledge at the top and complete ignorance and falsehood at the bottom. And our vocabulary of knowledge reflects this scale. We speak of knowledge, faith, opinion, supposition, educated guesses, probability, certainty, likelihood, etc. Absolute or perfect knowledge is held by God alone. Everything that is, is either God or an effect of God's action. And God knows his own being and action perfectly. God knows everything about everything. Human beings do not possess such knowledge. Does this mean that anything less than absolute knowledge is not knowledge at all, that human beings know nothing? Drawing this skeptical conclusion would imply that in relation to knowledge there is no qualitative difference between guesses, wishful thinking, prejudices, etc., and true, justified or warranted belief, no difference between science and superstition. I reject this view. I believe that our efforts to discover truth are worth the struggle.

What is Faith?

What is faith, and where does it fall on the scale of knowledge? A common misunderstanding opposes faith to knowledge. It assumes that to hold a belief by faith rules out its status as knowledge, and that to know something rules out its being held by faith. This opposition would be correct only if knowledge had to be defined as absolute knowledge. To say a belief is held on faith specifies that the believer has only indirect access to the reality to which the belief refers. The act of faith holds a belief to be true on the word of a trusted person or authority that has direct access to the reality in question. For example, to possess faith in the resurrection of Christ is to hold this belief to be true on the word of Paul, Peter, the Twelve and other witnesses to the resurrection appearances. Can such a belief be justified or warranted. Sure, it can. And, if it is true and justified or warranted, it counts as knowledge. There is no opposition between faith and knowledge. However there is a difference. One can *believe* falsehoods to be true, but one cannot *know* falsehoods to be true or truths to be false. Knowledge concerns how a *true* belief is held and faith concerns merely how a belief is held whether it is true or not.

The true counterpart to faith is intellectual or empirical intuition, not knowledge. Intuition has direct access to the reality it knows whereas faith has indirect access. We intuit logical and mathematical truths, and our senses make direct contact with the physical world. These intuitions produce beliefs. Logical deduction is slightly removed from intuition, and so its relation to reality is also indirect. It grasps the truth of a proposition through its logical relationships to other propositions that we hold to be true.

What is Opinion?

Like faith, opinion refers to an act of the knower and does not require the thing held as probably true to be really true. One forms an opinion by assessing the evidence for the truth of a proposition as weighty enough to make the proposition more likely true than not. In contrast, faith trusts the word of someone it believes really knows. In this sense, faith stands higher in the order of knowledge than opinion.

What is Certainty?

Certainty is a measure of the subjective purity with which a belief is held. A belief held with certainty by someone is beyond doubt to this person. They hold it with untroubled passion. However, certainty is not a measure of truth or knowledge. One can be certain that a falsehood is true or that a truth is false.

Are Christian Beliefs Knowledge, Opinion, Certainties Or Faith?

As we proceed in our study, we will see that many of the central Christian beliefs are held by faith. However, as I argued above, their being held by faith does not rule out their also being knowledge, that is, true, justified or warranted belief. Some Christian beliefs are supported by intellectual and empirical intuition. Some require a chain of logical reasoning. Other beliefs fall into the category of opinion. And Christians experience different levels of certainty in their faith at different times.

7

IS CHRISTIAN BELIEF A DECISION OR A CONCLUSION?

In the previous chapter we addressed the question of what it means to know something. I defined knowledge as true, justified or warranted, belief. It is important to note that this is merely a *definition* of knowledge. A definition of knowledge cannot tell us whether a particular belief is really true or whether a particular person is really justified or warranted in holding that belief. The definition can be applied to particular cases only hypothetically. If we accept the definition of knowledge as true, justified or warranted belief, it follows that: "If belief A is true and Susan is justified in holding A or possesses warrant for A, Susan knows A." But the definition gives us no way to get past the little word "if."

In other words, there is a huge difference between knowing A and knowing infallibly that you know A. (In my view, infallible knowledge is impossible apart from absolute knowledge.) And there is a huge difference between affirming the hypothetical statement, "If belief A is true and Susan is justified in holding A or possesses warrant for A, Susan knows A," and asserting categorically, "Susan knows A." In common speech, to say "I know A" asserts subjective certainty, and we learned in the previous chapter that subjective certainty is compatible with falsehood. And to assert that "Susan knows A" is to express a judgment that A is true and Susan is justified or warranted in holding A. Clearly, this judgment is also fallible.

Every human act asserting an existential statement of the form "A" or "A exists" or "The belief that A exists is true" is fallible. Even if the assertion is true and is held in a justified or warranted way, *the human act of judging the belief to be true is fallible.* We cannot infallibly rule out every possible condition under which a belief could be false. The universal fallibility of human judgments makes doubt a real possibility for any judgment. Doubt is the subjective side of fallibility and the subjective opposite of certainty. Doubt no more makes a belief false than certainty makes it true.

We adapt to human fallibility and doubt in much of our lives, especially in those areas where the consequences of being wrong are not severe. In purely theoretical matters—if there are such things—or practical matters of little consequence, we shrug our shoulders and say, "Who cares?" In those areas we are able rather easily and routinely to make decisions and act in the absence of infallibility and complete certainty. We do not notice that our judgments and the actions based on them are fallible and involve risk. But when the stakes are high and great good or great evil may result from our actions, we become acutely conscious of our fallibility. Subjective doubt and anxiety arise and may paralyze us unless we find a way to deal with them.

Now I want to apply these thoughts to our question, "Is Christianity True." If all human judgments are fallible and if in some really important matters, despite our best efforts to examine and weigh the evidence, we are forced to act on our fallible judgments, there will always come a point at which we must risk choosing, deciding and acting despite the risk. Hence in accounting for their Christian commitment, believers need not accept the obligation to "close the loop" and present conclusive proof for the truth of their faith. We can present the evidence and our evaluations of it, but we need not and cannot describe in rational terms the decision to act despite the risk. The necessity of acting on fallible judgments applies to all actions, trivial or monumental, enacted by believers and nonbelievers. Christian faith and commitment should not be held to a higher standard than other beliefs and commitments have to meet.

The necessity of decision and action based on responsible but fallible judgments determines much of my apologetic strategy and marks it off from many other approaches to apologetics. I hope to guide the reader on the road from unbelief to Christian faith. Along the way, we will come to four natural decision points where progress demands that we choose one of two ways in the absence of conclusive proof. I will do my best to clarify the nature of the alternatives, the evidence for and against each, and what is at stake in the decision between the two. But rational arguments can take us only so far. Finally, one must choose and act despite the risk.

Part Two

FOUR DECISION POINTS

In this section I will take us through four decision points on our way to full Christian faith. First, we must decide between atheism and belief in God. I argue that this decision depends on our choice between matter and mind as most fundamental explanation for our world. Is the beginning and end of all things spirit or matter, life or death, intelligible or unintelligible, mind or machine? Having decided that believing in God is the most rational choice, we will then confront the second decision point where we ask, "Is the mind that is evident in the intelligible order of the world impersonal or personal?" If we opt for a personal God, a third decision point confronts us with the choice between thinking of God as the highest aspect of nature or as transcendent over nature. Is God supernatural or natural? Is the world God's creation or God's body? The issue can also be framed as a decision between theism and panentheism, which is the idea that God is an aspect of the world neither wholly different from world nor fully identical to it. If we accept theism as the best answer to this third question, we come to the fourth decision point at which we must decide whether to remain mere theists or move into full Christian faith. At this crossroads we are required to discuss the possibility and actuality of a revelation of God in history. At the moment of decision we must assess the evidence for the bodily resurrection of Jesus Christ from the dead and reflect on the meaning of this event for the nature, identity and significance of Jesus.

8

THE PRIMAL CHOICE: DEAD MATTER OR LIVING MIND

I devoted the previous chapters to clarifying concepts needed to answer intelligently the question of Christianity's truth. We examined the nature of the question about Christianity's truth and the concepts of truth, reality, knowledge and faith. We dealt with the issue of who bears the burden of proof. Now we begin to address the heart of the matter.

Debates about the truth of Christianity begin at different points depending on which objection is being pressed. It would seem that a discussion with an atheist would need to begin with the question of God's existence. Deists would agree with Christians that God exists but would object to miracles, the incarnation and the resurrection of Jesus. And adherents of other religions and philosophies would press other objections and demand other bodies of evidence. Since in this book I am addressing a general audience, I don't want to presume a beginning point anywhere short of the most basic issue. In the previous chapter, I spoke of certain natural decision points at which one must decide which road to take. One road takes us further on the way to Christian faith and the other takes us another step away from faith. What is the first and most fundamental decision point?

If asked, perhaps most people would say that the most obvious beginning point for the debate between nonbelievers and believers is issue of the existence of God. Indeed, this debate may be the most obvious beginning point, but we must also keep in mind that explicit atheism and theism presuppose many judgments and decisions about background beliefs. These unspoken background beliefs must be true if atheism or theism is true. So, I want to look for the most fundamental decision point among these unspoken commitments.

Atheist philosophies vary markedly and resist simple generalizations. But I have to risk some generalizations or our argument would never progress beyond disputes over definitions. At this stage, using Alvin Plantinga's definition, I will define atheism as the belief that "there is no God or anything like God" *(Warranted Christian Belief)*. Theism is belief in one God conceived in a general sense that covers Christianity, Islam and Judaism. Perhaps some atheists would disagree, but I am going to take for granted that the debate about God's existence makes no sense unless atheists and theists alike believe that something is real, that something true can be said about it and that we can attain some knowledge of it. It would be hard to argue with someone who denies the presuppositions and rules that make arguments possible! In my view, a second assumption is needed to get the debate going. How could a debate progress unless atheists and theists agree that at the origin of all the manifold phenomena in the world lies something that explains the phenomena but itself needs no explanation? Rationality urges us to relate and unify things that seem at first unrelated and separate. The notion that ultimate reality is composed of an infinite number of unrelated, unconnected, utterly different and self-existent entities makes reason ineffective and knowledge impossible. Hence there is a tendency among atheists and theists to seek for the fewest and simplest explanatory principles possible.

We now have before us the first decision point. If atheists and theists agree that there is an ultimate reality that explains all phenomena and events, the debate turns on the nature of that ultimate reality. Is it spirit or matter, life or death, intelligible or unintelligible, mind or machine? Clearly, atheism, as the belief that there is no God or anything like God, chooses the second option in each of these four pairs. For atheism, the beginning and end of all things is matter, death, the unintelligible, and the mechanical. Theism chooses the first member of each pair. For theists, the beginning and end of all things is spirit, life, the intelligible and mind. The choice one makes at this fork in the road determines one's most basic understanding of everything else. All future choices are but specifications and variations of this one.

Is the choice between these two paths merely arbitrary or based on one's personality? Or, is there room for making rational judgments? And if so, what are our resources for making these rational judgments? I see only three: our experience of our minds, our experience of our bodies and our experience through our minds and bodies of the external world. Or, we can think of it this way: Through our bodies and minds we experience reality in two ways, as intelligible and unintelligible or as mental and material or clear and obscure or internal or external. These two basic experiences give us three options for relating matter and mind (1) the intelligible is primary and the material is derivative; or (2) the material is primary and the intelligible is derivative; or (3) the material and the intelligible are equally primordial.

9

THE MIRACLE OF ATHEISM: TURNING MATTER INTO MIND

In the previous chapter I argued that the first decision point in the discussion between atheism and belief in God is the choice between matter and mind as the most fundamental explanation for our world. Is the beginning and end of all things "spirit or matter, life or death, intelligible or unintelligible, mind or machine?" I ended with the question of whether or not we could make a rational judgment about this issue. Now I want to begin a line of reasoning that I believe enables us to reject materialism for rational reasons, not just because of our emotional reaction to its deification of death.

In this chapter we will consider a common experience central to the argument between atheism and belief. We experience ourselves and the external world in two ways, as mind and matter, that is, as something intelligible and as something merely sensible. We can think the intelligible as an idea, a concept or a set of relationships. The intelligible aspect of things enters our minds as information. But we experience the sensible as merely there, a brute fact offering resistance but not yielding information. Both are such primitive experiences that we can't readily explain one in terms of the other.

To move us forward, let's assume that the atheist option is correct, that matter is the one primordial reality, and see where this hypothesis leads us. If atheistic materialism is true everything we experience can be reduced to matter. Everything real is wholly material, and everything we experience as mind or idea is but an appearance of matter. By definition, pure matter cannot possess any intelligible properties. But can we actually perform this reduction of mind to matter?

To pursue this argument we need a clear concept of matter. But it would be a huge mistake to assume that our common sense notions give us an adequate concept of matter. Let's use a human artifact as our example of how the reduction of mind and intelligible ideas to matter might work. From the street in front of my house I can see the entire front of the structure. When I look at it I think the idea of a house. My house is not matter alone. Its matter is structured by an idea. The idea of a house contains many components we might consider practical or emotional, such as beauty, comfort, convenience and familiarity. But the idea of a house is also a complicated design plan that one can diagram as a set of blueprints and understand with the mind. The design plan differentiates the house from other physical objects, from a car or an elephant.

My house is composed of smaller units arranged according to its design plan. Let's remove one of those units and consider it in isolation from the other units. A single brick is not a house. Nor is pile of bricks a house. You need a design plan and a builder in addition to materials to create a house. But neither is a single brick pure matter, for there is a difference between a brick and unmixed, unmolded and unbaked clay. Not just any pile of earth can be made into a brick. Hence a brick, too, is an idea, a design plan, an inner order that makes its components a brick and not something else.

Let's go further. The brick also is composed of units arranged in an order, according to the idea of a brick. The units are composed mostly of Silicon and Aluminum oxides that possess properties that enable them to form tiny, thin, flat sheets, which gives wet clay that slick feel. Silicon tetraoxide molecules are also composed of units, one Silicon atom and four oxygen atoms. Single Silicon or single Oxygen atoms or an aggregate of these atoms is not a Silicon tetraoxide molecule any more than a brick is a house. And apart from the design plan that makes these atoms Silicon tetraoxide molecules, they do not possess the properties of Silicon tetraoxide.

A Silicon atom, too, is composed of units arranged in a stable and intelligible order. It contains 14 protons, 14 neutrons, and 14 electrons. Its inner structure is surprisingly complex, and a list of its known properties would fill several pages. In experiencing and understanding a Silicon atom, just like our knowledge and experience of a house or a brick, we do not experience matter alone. We know a Silicon atom as an order, an intelligible structure, that is, as an idea.

Let's keep going! A proton by itself is not a Silicon atom, and it does not possess the properties of a Silicon atom but a completely different set of properties. Like a house, a brick, Silicon tetraoxide molecules, and Silicon atoms, a proton is not pure matter. It too has an inner structure and is composed of units. A proton is composed of 2 up quarks and 1 down quark held together by three gluon fields. Quarks and gluons also possess properties that differ from those of the protons for which they are components. How far toward the infinitely small modern physics can pursue the structure and properties of the physical world I do not know. But one thing is clear: Matter, considered as primordial, unordered, unintelligible, undifferentiated stuff—a concept necessary for atheism to make sense—can never be known or experienced except as an abstraction from the ordered and intelligible world we know.

From our common sense experience of the world, we tend to think that the existence and nature of matter is the most obvious of things. And the immediate plausibility of argument for atheism depends on this naïve presumption. But the existence of matter is not obvious at all. Matter is a theoretical idea postulated to account for the difference between mere ideas and the physical objects that embody those ideas in space and time. Matter is not knowable in itself, that is, apart from an internally structured physical object. The physical order we experience daily is built up not from purely material components but by things with internal order, used as components for other orders, and those are used for still others and so on for many levels.

Nevertheless, let's continue to assume the materialist hypothesis. This hypothesis asserts that all the intelligible order in the universe, everything that ever was and ever will be, from quarks and gluons to human brains, came into existence not by the ordering power of mind but by some other means. What other means could account for the vast number of levels of intelligible order in nature? Apart from mind, what could be added to amorphous, unordered and undifferentiated matter to cause it to become ordered? If matter is all there is and matter is unordered by definition, why wouldn't matter simply remain unordered forever? Chance, you say? I agree that chance is the only option other than active mind for creating new order. But chance won't work to order pure matter, because chance applies only in our already ordered world. Chance makes sense only where there is differentiation and processes are already under way. Chance makes sense only where you have two or more lines of causality that can intersect in a way unpredictable from within either line. With pure matter there is no causal process because causal processes assume a difference between cause and effect, but in pure matter all is one and the same. Without difference nothing happens, and if nothing happens, nothing can happen by chance either. If, nevertheless, atheists insist that something did happen to order matter, they are asserting an absurdity, a miracle, which hardly places them a superior rational position to theists who insist that the operation of mind is the explanation for the intelligible order of our world.

As I stand before that first decision point, completely surrounded by intelligible structures, layer within layer, knowing matter only as an abstraction, I feel justified in rejecting the materialist alternative and choosing the alternative that asserts that mind and intelligibility are fundamental aspects of reality.

10

ATHEISM'S LEAP OF FAITH

In the preceding chapter we pursued the hypothesis of materialism from the starting point of our experience of the world through the senses. We experience the external world as structured in intelligible ways we can understand through common sense and natural science. But we also experience it as external, as brute facts offering only resistance to penetration by mind or body. But as we examined physical objects we discovered that we can break them apart to experience their internal order as intelligible. We were unable to discover pure matter through the senses. Every object we thought might be pure matter ended up being internally structured and therefore at least partially intelligible, that is, partly an idea. Matter, we concluded, is the abstract idea of an unintelligible, unordered, yet real stuff we can never experience apart from its connection with intelligible structure.

Now I want us to begin our examination of materialism at another point. We experience ourselves as creators and causes, as initiators of movement and change. We possess a first person consciousness of ourselves as actors, as free. We are able freely to create information and through our bodies shape the material world according to this information. In other words, we experience ourselves not only as passive readers of information encoded in physical objects but also as active minds, wills and creative powers.

Of course, some materialists deny that we really are active minds that can initiate change and create information. We are merely part of the material process of cause and effect. But those materialists who deny freedom always base their denial on their theory, as one of its implications. They never deny that it seems to our own consciousness that we are free and creative. In my view, denying what *seems* self-evident to consciousness because of one's commitment to materialist theory strains credulity and calls into ques-tion the denier's commitment to rationality. What can you say to someone who denies what we and they cannot help but believing? I view this denial as on the level with some-one who denies the existence of the external world. Our experience of freedom is as primitive and irreducible as the experience we gain from the senses. We cannot verify one by the other or reduce one to the other.

Materialists, too, must begin with trust. They must trust the senses to tell them the truth about the existence and nature of matter. Such primitive experiences cannot be verified by more basic experiences, for there are none. But in order to be rationally responsible adherents of any theory about the external world, including materialism, we have to believe that we have minds capable of taking the data from the senses and constructing a true theory. It seems to me, then, that affirming the truth of materialism requires also affirming the irreducible reality of free and creative minds; yet these two affirmations are clearly incompatible.

What does it mean to say that mind and intelligibility are real? Most people have no trouble believing that something is real when they can experience it with one of the five senses. More precisely, we believe things are real if there are any possible circumstances under which they can be experienced, even if those means are not yet available to us. Even more generally, *we consider something real if it possesses causal power*, that is, if there are any possible circumstances under which it can effect change in something else or be changed or resist being changed by something else. We cannot know a "thing" that possesses no causal power, and we do not consider it real. When we think of it this way, we can see that our minds, our ideas and the ideas that structure nature are *real*. We experience their causal power. Our minds create information, which can in combination with physical power create new things in the external world. New ideas arising from our own creativity or from other minds or from natural objects inform our minds, that is, they cause change in our minds. *Hence, if to be real means to possess causal power, our minds, their ideas and the ideas that give the world its intelligibility are certainly real...just as real as stuff that creates change in our senses.*

I think I am on solid ground, then, when I assume that our experience of ourselves as free causes of movement and change and free creators of new information tells us the truth. Not only do we experience in our own being a mind capable of abstracting and thinking the information that structures the external world, we experience directly our minds as active and creative. Just as I experience my feelings of pain or pleasure or fear as self-evident and undeniable, I also experience myself as a free cause with the same certainty. We make a difference between the automatic unconscious processes that go on within our bodies and our deliberate choices and acts. We know the difference between being knocked to the ground by the impact of a physical object and our deliberate act of sitting down. There is a qualitative difference between the two.

In the previous chapter I showed that we cannot imagine a rational way to account for the intelligible order's genesis from pure, amorphous, undifferentiated matter. For the reasons I mentioned there, chance can't do the job. Other than active mind the only option is the sheer absurdity of asserting that it happened, somehow, anyway. But why choose the absurdity of spontaneous generation when we experience our own minds as free causes able to initiate change, create information and place it into a physical medium? We know this can happen because we actually do it! Hence we have a simple, rational explanation for the intelligible structure that permeates nature: Active mind is at least equally primordial with matter.

We do not need to resort to an arbitrary leap of faith made necessary by commitment to the metaphysical theory of reductive materialism.

Now we have a second rational reason to reject the materialist option. We can take the road that affirms the irreducible and primordial nature of mind, intelligibility, life and spirit.

11

GOD, MATTER AND OTHER MINDS

In the past two chapters we examined a background belief that must be true if atheism is true, that is, that matter is the ultimate reality that explains the existence and nature of everything else. We evaluated this materialist option from two different experiential starting points, our experience of the intelligibility and materiality of the external world and our experience of our own minds as active, free and creative. Now we will consider materialism from a third experiential starting point: our experience other minds, other intelligent human persons.

Amazingly, we can understand and think ideas that come from other human minds. We find ourselves not only able to read passive information written into nature and able to write information into the physical world; we also encounter other minds like ours, active, free and able to communicate information from their minds to ours through language. Although there is no way to prove that a human body with whom we are speaking really possesses a mind like ours, we believe it so strongly that we think it absurd to doubt it. We recognize in others what we experience as self-evident in ourselves. What does our experience of other minds, that is, other intelligent human persons, add to our experience of the intelligibility of the physical world and of ourselves as active minds?

First, the existence of other minds confirms our internal experience of ourselves as active, free and creative minds. Our experience of freedom, which *seems* so real experienced from inside, is confirmed as *really* real in encounter with other people who act and express that same freedom. Our mental encounter with other minds differs from decoding the structures embedded in the physical world. In our efforts to understand the intelligible order in the physical world we experience the order as passive and ourselves as active. But when we meet other minds we find that they are also active and creative. In encounters with other people we experience being understood by the thing that we are attempting to understand. We meet a new kind of reality, a person. Other minds/persons actively resist and protest any effort to reduce them to their ideas, sense impressions or material constituents. We also resist and protest such depersonalization. And, in encountering other persons we become aware of our own irreducible personhood more intensely than we can in encountering the passive intelligible order in the physical world.

Second, the existence of other human minds and our ability to communicate with each other adds a new dimension to our experience of intelligibility within the physical world. Our minds meet and transfer information through the medium of the external world in which we find an intelligible order that can be understood alike by many minds. In verbal language we encode information in the medium of air as sound impulses. Receiving information from another person through language gives us confidence that we know what the other is thinking, and we know it by rethinking the thought communicated.

Our experience of other minds as free actors and creators of information and as co-readers of the information encoded in the physical world reinforces our conviction that the order that structures the physical world is indeed intelligible and derives from an active mind. We experience minds other than our own creating information understandable by us and still other minds.

Third, encountering other intelligent persons introduces a moral dimension to our experience of mind, a sense of the inestimable worth of others. Such encounters introduce the idea that the universe is ordered not only in increasing levels of complexity but also in increasing levels of value, which in turn gives birth to the idea of a teleological order that moves toward producing greater and greater perfection.

Does our experience of other minds/persons add anything to the case made in the previous two chapters for choosing the option that affirms the irreducible and primordial nature of mind, intelligibility, life and spirit and for rejecting materialism? Yes, I think it does. (1) In the previous chapter I argued that our experience of our own minds gives plausibility to active mind as the explanation for the intelligible order in the world. Encountering other free and creative persons strengthens our conviction that our minds are irreducible to matter. Hence our experience of active minds/persons other than our own reinforces the idea that a primordial active mind orders the world. (2) Our experience of other minds/persons opens up a moral and teleological dimension to our experience of the world. These dimensions cannot be perceived simply by using our reason to read the information embedded in the physical world or experiencing ourselves as creators of information. If the worth we perceive in other persons is a real property, independent of our subjective feelings, this worth must be the product of a valuing and purposive mind at least equally primordial with matter.

In the next chapter we will summarize the case for moving through the first decision point on the road from nonbelief to Christian faith. Though we cannot remove all possible doubt, we will take the road marked "Mind is at Least Equally Primordial with Matter" and leave untraveled the road marked "Matter is the Ultimate Reality that Explains Everything Else." Now we are faced with the second decision point: is the mind that orders the world one or many, personal or impersonal?

12

TIME FOR DECISION

In the previous three chapters we have been standing before first decision point on path from nonbelief to Christian faith. We must decide whether mind or matter is the ultimate reality that explains the existence and nature of everything else. Belief in God presupposes the background belief that mind is at least as fundamental as matter, and atheism presupposes that matter alone is fundamental and explains everything else. If it could be shown that matter is the final explanation for mind and all mind-like features of the universe, belief in God would be defeated. If, on the other hand, mind could be shown to be at least as ultimate as matter, atheism would be defeated.

I argued from three different experiences that it is eminently reasonable to believe that mind is as necessary to explain the world of our experience as matter is. We examined our experience of the intelligibility of the external order of nature. In our analysis we found no way to reduce the intelligible order of nature to pure, unordered matter, and we rejected chance as the explanation for that order. Afterward, we considered our experience of ourselves as initiating causes and creators of information. We argued from this experience that it is reasonable to believe that an active universal mind gives the world its intelligible order. Finally, we argued that our experience of other minds "strengthens our conviction that our minds are irreducible to matter. Hence our experience of active minds/persons other than our own reinforces the idea that a primordial, active mind orders the world."

We could dwell here forever endlessly debating the many issues involved in the choice between mind and matter as the ultimate reality. We could ask, "How can mind emerge from pure matter? How can immaterial mind exercise causality on a material world?" But now it is time to decide. I am convinced that further discussions would not settle the issue definitively. There is no hope that further investigation would bring forward indubitable proof for one alternative or the other and remove the necessity for a fallible decision. The best we can hope for is a decision based on reasonable and responsible judgments. And I believe the three arguments we have considered make reasonable our belief that mind is at least as ultimate as matter and make responsible our decision to act on this belief.

Since there are no definitive arguments for either side, some would argue that a stance of agnosticism and indecision is the most rational position. This argument contends that agnosticism's subjective uncertainty and indecision corresponds to the objective situation of our lack of absolute knowledge whereas a decision to build one's life and worldview on either alternative goes beyond the evidence. And cultivating certainty and plunging into action beyond the reach of the evidence abandons reason in favor of irrational impulse.

I don't think I need to enter an extended discussion of agnosticism at this point, but I'd like to make two points in response to the argument in the previous paragraph. First, one cannot be agnostic about everything. In the argument above the agnostic makes the judgment that both the evidence for and the evidence against materialism are inadequate to justify knowledge claims and decisive actions. This agnostic judgment possesses all the qualities of other judgments: it is fallible or infallible, true or false and genuine knowledge or not. If the agnostic judgment rises to the level of genuine knowledge, the agnostic must abandon agnosticism at least on this issue. If the judgment in question is fallible, the agnostic loses the right to criticize atheism or theism for going beyond the evidence; the agnostic also acts on the basis of fallible judgments. Second, some decisions are so fundamental to the act of living that they cannot be avoided or postponed. Perhaps, I need never form a definitive judgment about whether or not intelligent life exists somewhere in the Milky Way galaxy. I can think of no practical difference my opinion on the subject would make. But we cannot avoid the decision between atheism and belief in God. If we live at all or do anything at all, we must live and act on one belief or another. For these beliefs define the origin, destiny, meaning and purpose of human life. And these limits determine everything in between, defining the distinctions between good and evil, right and wrong and the worthwhile and the useless. The rationality of every human act or decision not to act will be judged by its consistency with these ideas. In the case of agnosticism, refusing to decide is to decide to act as if we could live without acting, a huge self-deception.

But I have argued that the decision to reject materialism in favor of belief is quite rational. Once we make this decision—especially since we see that further discussion would not change the necessity of making a fallible decision—we need not look back in doubt. We can move forward to build our thoughts on the foundation of reasonable judgments and responsible decisions made at the first decision point. We can now presuppose the existence of a universal mind that manifests itself in the intelligible order of the world. This forward-looking boldness will characterize each of the decision point transitions we make on the way to Christian faith. These points are watershed moments where one must take risks to move forward into decisive action. We are being prepared for the most demanding decision, the move into faith in Jesus Christ.

13

IS GOD OR HUMANITY THE SUPREME BEING?

In this chapter we leave behind the first decision point on the path to Christian faith. Having made a reasonable and responsible decision to affirm the irreducible reality of mind and to attribute the intelligible order of the physical world to an active and universal mind, we now need to consider the nature of that mind. In the most general sense, the issue can be stated as follows: "Is the mind that is evident in the intelligible order of the world impersonal or personal?" More specifically, is the mental aspect of reality an unconscious, primitive urge that drives evolution toward higher and higher order culminating in self-conscious human beings? Or, in another impersonal option, is the universal mind a kind of logical necessity, impersonal in itself, that develops automatically into a world that contains finite, self-conscious minds like ours? Or, in a third option on impersonal side of the second decision point, does the universal mind possess a primitive consciousness—not yet self-conscious, personal and free—that itself evolves into god. In this theory, God was not always as great as God is now and did not create the world in a sovereign and free decision; instead, God grows and becomes greater in a world process that includes God and matter evolving together according to impersonal laws not subject to God's choice.

To consider the personal alternative in the second decision point, we ask, "Is God always and forever personal?" Obviously the term "personal" is derived from our experience in ourselves and other human beings of those qualities that distinguish us from nonliving things and life on a lower level. In contrast to other things, we possess self-consciousness, knowledge, freedom and capacity for interpersonal relationships. Only if God's possess these qualities may we think of God as powerful, loving, merciful, communicative, responsive and purposive. Only a personal God can create the world and accompany it to God's intended destination. Only a personal God can hear our prayers, know our names, exercise providence in our lives and guarantee that will we reach our God-given destination. Only a personal God can root our personal identity in an eternal reality and ground our worth in divine love. Only if God is personal can Christianity be true.

But which alternative conception of God makes the most sense, an impersonal god or a personal God? I have conversed with people who deny being atheists but insist that they cannot believe in "a personal God." My first reaction to such a qualification is a bit flippant: isn't the notion of an impersonal god a contradiction? Why would you call an impersonal process "God"? Isn't this a rather confusing use of the word God? Why not say that you do not believe in God at all? Sometimes, I get the impression that people who claim not to believe in a personal God are not expressing the conclusion of a serious thought project; rather, they are expressing their feelings of discomfort with the idea of God. But let's assume that those who think of god as impersonal believe something like one of the three alternatives I described above: God is an urge, a logical necessity or the goal of evolution.

Consider the following implications of the assertion that god is impersonal. To think of God as impersonal in one of these three senses is to insinuate that the god that produced us exists on a lower level of being than we do. Humanity is the highest level of being the world has yet attained. The implications of such a claim are rather eye opening. If god is impersonal, we know more than god does. We understand ourselves better than god understands "his" being. Indeed, we understand god better than god does. We are freer than god. We possess every noble, powerful and desirable quality to a higher degree than god does. God doesn't even know that "he" exists. Let me put it bluntly. We deserve the title "god" much more than an impersonal process does, however ancient, primitive and productive that process may be. And the deification of human self-consciousness may be the secret within the idea of an impersonal god. Humanity is highest manifestation to date of the world process, and "God" is our imaginary image of the end stage of the world process.

The choice between a personal and an impersonal god, we can now see, is a choice between believing that there exists something infinitely greater and better than we are or believing that we are the greatest and best existing beings. My intuition is that human beings possess an inner tendency to believe that there must exist something much greater and better than humanity, since that "Something" produced beings as amazing as us. How disappointing it would be to discover that we are the Supreme Being, that this is as good as it gets!

14

AN IMPERSONAL GOD?

In the previous chapter we pursued the question of whether it makes sense to think of the mind that gives the world its intelligible order as impersonal. Can we reasonably think of that mind as a primitive urge, a logical necessity or the goal of evolution? We ended that chapter by observing the counterintuitive nature of belief in an impersonal god. How can we believe that the universal mind that gives the world its intelligible order and that produces human beings does not itself possess the qualities that make human beings personal: self-consciousness, reason, freedom and the ability to relate to other persons?

Now I want to make a bit more explicit our intuitive belief that the mind that produced the world is much greater and better than we are. Let's remember our earlier argument for the irreducibility of the intelligible aspect of nature and for a universal mind that is the explanation for that intelligibility. We argued from our own experience of ourselves as free causes and originators of information that mind is a better explanation for the intelligible order in nature than chance is. The decision for a universal mind was prompted by our intuition that information always originates from the free act of an intelligent agent. And free acts always involve self-awareness and are always enacted to achieve ends. Hence the assertion that the universal mind is impersonal contradicts the original reason for rejecting materialism and accepting the irreducible reality of mind. To deny that the power that forms the world into an intelligible order is free, reasonable, self-aware and able to relate to others is to retreat from our first decision point and fall back into materialism.

To think of the universal mind as impersonal is to confuse mind with ideas or concepts. Indeed, ideas and concepts are not intelligent and free. They are objects the mind creates and thinks. My previous argument for the irreducible nature of the intelligibility in the world did not contend that the intelligible order is itself personal. It contended, rather, that the universal, intelligible order is the *product* an active, universal mind. And the mind responsible for *creating* the intelligible order of the universe must be free, reasonable and self-aware to a degree far beyond human beings. If that "mind" were impersonal, it could not *produce* anything; instead, it would itself need to be produced. And we would simply be mistaken in using the word "mind" to designate the impersonal order that evolved by chance.

To think of God as impersonal sees God as in some way embedded in or limited by matter, perhaps, in analogy to the way we are embodied. Our bodies carry on many of their organic functions independently of our will or even our awareness. Many of our feelings and urges arise involuntarily. But again, refer to my original argument for the universal mind. The universal mind must be responsible for the *entire* intelligible order or the argument fails. But asserting that the universal mind is embodied in matter implies that this mind cannot be responsible for *all* the intelligible order, because if it were so embodied it would not be responsible for itself, its own embodiment or the laws that govern that relationship. We would have to face again the prospect of materialism, that is, underneath the intelligible aspects of nature rests a non-intelligible cause working by blind processes to produce all natural phenomena.

The intuitive assumption that drives our argument is an ancient one clearly articulated by Aristotle and used in theology by Thomas Aquinas: *actuality is prior in the order of being to potentiality.* It is intuitive because we experience it in ourselves and in our observations of the world. Only actual, living minds produce information. A cause imposes its (actual) likeness on the effect to make it actual. Order produces order. True chaos never changes. The intuition that actuality is prior to potentiality makes it impossible to believe that the amazing intelligible order in the universe arose from absolute disorder by chance. The mind that orders the world must itself be purely actual, possessing maximum order.

The most reasonable conclusion available to us at this point—given our assumption that a universal mind is the cause of the intelligible order of nature—is that God is pure, active mind completely independent of matter. But if God is pure, active mind, God must be maximally free, self-aware, rational and able to relate, that is, personal to the highest degree.

15

"I'M SPIRITUAL BUT NOT RELIGIOUS"

How often have you heard it? "I'm spiritual but not religious." More than a few times, I suspect. And it's hard to know what to say to this self-designation. So, let's think about it.

We've been discussing the issue of an impersonal God from a theoretical point of view. This chapter provides an opportunity to look at it from a practical angle. Increasingly in recent years, people claim to be "spiritual" but not "religious." I've wanted to subject this idea to analysis for some time, and I am happy that it fits in the book.

It's not easy to specify what people mean when they affirm the importance of spirituality but deny their need for religion. In many cases I get the impression that the person making the distinction doesn't have a clear idea either. Perhaps their negation of religion is stronger and clearer in their minds than their affirmation of spirituality. Popular culture has largely succeeded in portraying religion and highly religious people as narrow-minded, ignorant, intolerant, judgmental, exclusive and more than a little neurotic. When people deny being religious their main concern may be to make a statement about their own character by differentiating themselves from the cultural image of the religious person. For some people, the "spiritual but not religious" claim is simply a less obviously self-commending way of saying "I am a good person, tolerant and welcoming, unlike those bad people, who are judgmental and reactionary. You will like me." They use the self-designation "spiritual" because the culture has settled on this term to designate an open, welcoming, tolerant, inclusive, progressive, sensitive and slightly mystical attitude. You can be spiritual even if you are somewhat agnostic or incline toward atheism, as long as you possess those soft and sensitive qualities listed above. Popular culture rejects harsh and militant atheism for the same reason it rejects judgmental religion.

Why use the term "spiritual"? Popular use of this term derives ultimately from the New Testament's teaching about the Holy Spirit. From its beginning, Christianity has understood God's presence and action in the world in a Trinitarian way. Father, Son and Spirit are one in being and their action is always united, but each is especially associated with certain activities: the Father with creation, the Son with salvation and the Spirit with transformation of the inner life of the believer. Because the Spirit's work always points to the Father and the Son, the Spirit has been called the anonymous member of the Trinity. Perhaps more importantly for the subject we are discussing, the Spirit's work is mysterious, internal and experiential.

In Christian history, the Spirit is identified with the inner divine presence that is often manifested in wordless mystical experience of union with the divine, euphoric feelings of joy or loss of control of the body. The writings of Christian mystics are often called "spiritual writings," and the study of these writings is called "spiritual theology." Spiritual authors record experiences of visions of Christ, overwhelming feelings of divine presence, inspirations from the Spirit and other intense experiences of the divine. Sometimes mystics strayed outside the bounds of orthodox Christian doctrine, but mostly they were able to thrive alongside traditional teaching. But during the modern era, especially with the help of the Romantic Movement of the late 18th and the early 19th centuries, Christian spirituality and pietism were for some people de-Christianized and assimilated to pantheism or vague nature mysticism.

When contemporary people say "I'm spiritual but not religious" they are unknowingly continuing this romantic tradition and its dislike of responsibility to the personal God of Christian faith. Christian religious practice focuses on a personal God, the God whose identity is delineated in the biblical narratives and in the life of Jesus Christ. In the Bible, the character and will of God are clear and determinate. God is not "whatever you understand him to be." God demands our loyalty, love and obedience. The first command of the Decalogue is "You shall have no other gods before me." Jesus said, "You cannot serve two masters." And one of the earliest Christian confessions of faith is "Jesus in Lord." Not a vague spirituality!

The contemporary move into "spirituality" attempts to escape the perceived negative aspects of belief in a personal God without giving up its positive aspects. Such concepts as truth, law, responsibility, discipleship, obedience and other restrictive concepts strike many of our contemporaries as exclusive, judgmental and harsh. And adopting a "spiritual" philosophy allows one to root one's life in a mysterious universe friendly to human life and values without the drawback of responsibility to a personal God. Ultimately, however, such spirituality, apart from belief in a personal God, leads to divinization of the human spirit or even of the individual self. "Spirituality" resonates perfectly with contemporary therapeutic culture, which makes not salvation and truth but the momentary feeling of wellbeing its highest aspiration.

16

IS GOD THE MIND AND CONSCIENCE OF NATURE?

We've been considering the second decision point on the road toward Christian faith, that is, the choice between an impersonal and a personal God. In this instance as with all the decision points on this journey we cannot be compelled to choose the option that moves us closer to Christianity. Nor can I claim to have proved the existence of a personal God beyond any doubt. As I have insisted all along, our judgments in these areas are fallible and we cannot exclude all risk from our decisions. Nevertheless, I believe that this judgment is reasonable and the decision to live consistently with it is responsible.

Before we move into the third decision point, I'd like to clear up a possible misunderstanding. I am not arguing that this path and these exact decision points must be followed in the order I outline before one can legitimately accept Christianity as true. This path treats the background beliefs that must be true if Christianity is true. It follows an order in which philosophers often treat these questions, an order of priority in being that moves from things that seem basic and necessary to those that appear derivative and contingent. One need not examine these beliefs or even become aware of them to come to Christian faith. People have moved from atheism to belief in God by encountering the beauty and wonder of the universe or the depths of human love. One can be moved from atheism to Christian faith simply by listening to the gospel of Jesus Christ. You don't need to work your way out of materialism by reason alone or get beyond the idea of an impersonal god solely by intellectual means. But if you come to believe in God and Jesus Christ by hearing the gospel or experiencing love, it still remains true that you implicitly accept all the background beliefs that cohere with this decision. You cannot believe in a personal God and believe that matter is the ultimate explanation for all reality. Nor can you believe in gospel of Jesus Christ and believe in an impersonal god.

My hope is that thinking through this argument step-by-step will help nonbelievers by showing that the background beliefs that make atheism plausible are questionable, if not simply false. If I can show that materialism is flawed or false, atheism is undermined even if the immediate motive for denying God's existence is the presence of evil in the world. Showing that the idea of an impersonal god is incoherent may motivate the "spiritual but not religious" group to seek a relationship with the personal God and hence be open to full Christian faith. Believers can also benefit from following the path I'm tracing. Making explicit and seeing the truth of Christianity's background beliefs may strengthen the believer's conviction that judgments in favor of Christianity's truth can be reasonable and decisions to follow the Christian way can be responsible.

The Third Decision Point

The third decision point confronts us with the choice between thinking of God as the highest aspect of nature or as transcending nature. Is God supernatural or natural? Is the world God's creation or God's body? The issue can also be framed as a decision between theism and panentheism. (Panentheism is the theory that God and the world of our experience are two aspects the one ultimate reality.) Before we go into this discussion, perhaps I ought to say that we are getting close to the limits of what we can achieve by reasoning from our experience of the natural world and our own minds. If God really transcends the world and our minds as their Creator, there can be no natural continuity between us and God. Our reasoning can at best take us to the limits of nature and to the limits of what is given with our minds. It cannot take us beyond them. Reason can follow natural law to its limits, but if there is a reality not subject to natural law, we cannot find it in this way.

Nevertheless, there is work for reason to do even at this point. If we begin with the presumption that God is intelligent, personal and free—a conclusion we reached in the first two decision points—we can examine the reasonableness of thinking of God as a part of nature, subject to basic natural law. If we find this view of God incoherent or inadequate to experience or intuitively unsatisfying, we may find the alternative of a transcendent Creator attractive. And even though we cannot reason directly from our experience of nature and our minds to a transcendent God, we may be willing to consider other ways in which we can achieve such knowledge. If we cannot ascend to God on the ladder of reason, perhaps God can descend to us. If God transcends the laws of the natural world God has created, why should we think the limits nature places on us apply also to God?

17

THE LIMITS OF REASON AND DIVINE REVELATION

Reason has limits. We can reason only from what is given to the senses or the mind. We can extend our knowledge of the empirical world by tracing the causal connections among the data given to the senses. Our knowledge of the mental world can be expanded by tracing the connections among the ideas and concepts given with the mind. But reason cannot reach beyond what is given to it except, perhaps, in its sense of not being able to grasp its own existence. When we reason about any natural object given to us, we feel in control of our power to understand it. We feel even more in control when we construct an artificial object. But when we turn our minds to the question of the origin and existence of the mind itself, we find no object given to reason that could be subjected to reason's power. Reason confronts its limits in its experience of not being able to grasp the ground of its own existence and powers. Reason operates powerfully within the limits of naturally given objects, but when confronted with the question of its own origin, it faces a mystery beyond its comprehension.

Unless this Mystery freely itself reveals itself to reason, our thinking about it will be limited to speculation based on decisions about which analogies to press into the unknown. In previous chapters, I labeled these decisions about analogies "decision points." At the first decision point we had to decide whether to conceive of the unknown ground of our existence as matter or mind. We chose mind. The second decision point forced us to choose between an impersonal and a personal God. We chose a personal God. The third decision point now confronts us with the choice between a personal God who is interdependent with the natural world and a personal God who is completely independent and transcendent over the natural world.

Why would any modern western person think of God as part of the world, just as dependent on the world as the world is on God? As far as I can tell, thinkers who view God this way share the presupposition that everything that is real in any sense falls within the sphere of reason's natural space. We can reason our way into the divine nature from what is naturally given to the mind and the senses. Hence nature's most fundamental laws apply equally to God and nature, and the concepts, propositions and words used to understand nature apply to God in a literal sense. Allow me to depart from my usual practice and quote two twentieth-century thinkers who express this view quite clearly. Alfred North Whitehead stated his central axiom in these words: "God is not to be treated as an exception to all metaphysical principles, invoked to save their collapse. He is their chief exemplification" [*Process and Reality: An Essay in Cosmology* (New York: Macmillan, 1929), p. 521]. Charles Hartshorne asserts that "theology (so far as it is the theory of the essence of the deity) is the most literal of all sciences of existence...the pure theory of divinity is literal, or it is a scandal, neither poetry nor science, neither well reasoned nor honestly dispensing with reasoning" *(Divine Relativity,* pp. 36-37). Hence God is continuous with nature.

But when we follow the logic of those who think God must be continuous with nature, the resulting picture of God differs dramatically from the traditional Jewish and Christian view of God. God evolves, learns and grows along with the rest of nature. God is not eternal but bound to time and space. God does not know the future and knows the past only by remembering it. Although God is infinite in potential, he is finite in actual existence. God did not create the world from nothing and is not all-powerful. God acts only by persuasion and never gets all he wills. Miracles make no sense because the laws of nature bind God as much as they bind us.

I think it is fair to ask whether the word God should be used of such a being. Before the rise of Christianity, in the Ancient Near East or Greece and Rome, the word "god" could be used of such a limited being. But most people under the influence of Christian theology would reserve the word God for the being than "which nothing more excellent or exalted exists" (Augustine, *Confessions*). Even more definitively, Anselm of Canterbury urged, "God is that, than which nothing greater can be conceived." How can we think of God as a being that could in reality or in thought be surpassed in excellence and perfection—even by himself?

Now we return to the thought with which we began this chapter: reason has limits. Given reason's lack of self-comprehension and its inability to comprehend its origin and ground, it is reasonable for reason to look for something beyond nature and its laws that can serve as their ground and explanation. Though such an act cannot be deduced or predicted by natural reason, it makes sense to maintain openness for the divine mystery to reveal itself within our sphere. And Christianity claims that this revelation really happened, and its view of God is definitively determined by its understanding of this revelation.

18

WHO IS GOD? IS THERE A WAY TO KNOW?

How do you decide between Christianity and some other form of theism? Up to this point in the book we've limited ourselves to reasoning from what is given always and everywhere to reason. We reasoned from the appearances of the natural world given through the senses and from the mind's knowledge of itself gained by internal reflection to the ultimate explanation for the existence and operations of these things. Using these sources, we confronted three decision points where we had to make a choice between two explanations for our experience: (1) matter or mind, (2) an impersonal or a personal God and (3) God as a part of nature or God as wholly transcending nature. The cumulative argument of the book so far amounts to this: believing in a personal God that wholly transcends nature can be based on a reasonable judgment and a responsible decision. I do not claim to have proved this conclusion beyond all doubt. I have not presented every argument for God's existence or attempted to refute every argument against it. But I have presented what I believe to be the reasoning mind's own drive toward God as the only explanation that does it justice. At this point, I must let the evidence speak for itself and move on.

The Fourth Decision Point

What is the first step one must take to transition from mere theism to Christian faith? As I admitted in previous chapters, I don't think there is only one path from unbelief to Christian faith. Different people make the transition differently. The order I wish to propose here makes sense to me because it addresses some concerns of our age and considers the questions our culture asks of Christians. If you can think of a better one, by all means follow it.

How does the Christian message enter the sphere of our reason so that we can assess its meaning and make a judgment about its truth? Clearly it is not given everywhere and always with nature. Nor is Christianity built into the structure of our minds. Hence Christianity is not merely a metaphysical explanation of the workings of nature or our minds. Nor can its coherence and truth be judged only by its conformity with these perennially present structures. From where then does the information on which we can base a rational judgment and a responsible decision about Christianity come? Is there another source for truth relevant to the question of God and the appropriate human relationship to God? Or must our knowledge of God be derived solely from structures perennially available to us in nature or mind? (Deism insists on this limit.)

Two other options come to mind: (1) divine illumination or inspiration of every individual or (2) a unique event in history, a record of which is passed on in language to those not present at the event. I do not wish to deny the possibility or even an actual event of illumination or inspiration of individuals. After all, Saul of Tarsus (Paul the Apostle) claims to have experienced the resurrected Jesus Christ in a unique vision or revelation. And others since his time have made similar claims and experienced similar conversions. But I don't think this is the norm. Today and for centuries past, most people meet the events on which Christianity is based in the form of language, that is, reports of the founding events that claim to derive from those who actually witnessed them.

Before we look at those reports, I want us to think about history as a source of information. By "history" I do not mean history in its proper sense. The "history" of historians is a reconstructed narrative of events based on critical assessment of the sources that claim to have access to that event. For the historian, neither events themselves nor reports of events are "history" in the technical sense. But at this point I want to use the word history loosely to mean the entire fabric of past events. Natural scientists assume that past natural events and processes—though unique in their particular time and place and order— operated by the same physical laws as natural events and processes operate today. The eruption of Vesuvius in AD 79 was a unique natural event, but we assume that it can be explained by same physical laws that operate everywhere and at all times in the universe. In a sense, each natural event is new and unique and cannot be repeated exactly. But these new and unique natural events do not reveal new natural laws. Only when natural events are brought into relationship with human and divine actions do they acquire the potential to reveal anything beyond natural law.

For the rest of this chapter, I will use the term "history" to designate the complex flow of human actions and passions and interactions through time. In human history we see something we do not see in natural history, genuine novelty fueled by human freedom. I recognize that human beings' free decisions are set in the context of certain stable features of human biology, psychology and sociology and in relation to natural history. But I deny that human history can be explained wholly by such deterministic factors. Writing, art, architecture, cities, poetry and philosophy are in part products of human freedom and not merely determinations of the laws of nature. Because of the activity of human freedom, history is the realm of the new and unique. And the most significant of those new and unique things is the unique personhood of each individual human being. There never was and there never will be another Julius Caesar, Paul the Apostle, Abraham Lincoln or you.

Why are other people fascinating to us? Even though each person possesses a unique identity we cannot share, we can see in their stories realizations of possibilities, free actions and sufferings that could be ours. Each person's life history is a revelation of something humanity could be, of what you and I could be. Hence history may embody and the study of history may reveal something the study of nature and of the mind cannot get at: the possibilities of the human spirit both to create and become something that transcends the possibilities of the ordinary course of nature. Only in human history is such a revelation possible. It cannot be known abstractly because it is the product of freedom. It can be known only in its actual realization, and since the actual realization of personal identity happens in human individuals, we can come to know it only through personal revelation expressed in their acts, creations and language. To know persons from the past we must rely on their stories recorded and passed down.

What if one individual realized the possibilities of human nature and freedom so completely and dramatically that this person's life became the definitive revelation of human destiny and of divine identity? This is exactly what Christianity claims for Jesus Christ.

19

CHRISTIAN FAITH: OUTSIDER VERSUS INSIDER VIEWS

As we concluded in the previous chapter, we cannot move from mere theism into Christian faith by reasoning from the phenomena of nature to their metaphysical cause or from the inner world of our minds and their ideas to necessary truths about God. At best, these routes can take us to theism as a reasonable explanation for our experience. Though Christianity shares many background beliefs in common with theism, it appeals to specific events within human history as the basis for its identifying truth claims. In an interesting and controversial move that I will need to defend in future chapters, Christianity sees revealed in these unique and non-repeating historical events truths of universal significance and application: truths about the identity and purposes of God, truths about the human condition in relation to God and truths about ultimate human destiny. For now, however, we will address a question preliminary to this issue.

Where do we learn about these historical events and truth claims? I am not asking the question of how we know these events really happened and these claims are true. It's too early to talk about this issue. I am asking a prior question: how do we get into the position of needing to evaluate and decide about the reports of the events and the truth claims derived from them? The simple answer is that we read about them in the scriptures of the Old and New Testaments. However, we are not looking for the simplest answer but for the most accurate and persuasive description of the move from not believing to believing Christianity. And this means that we must distinguish between insider and outsider views of these reports.

For Christian believers, the scriptures of the Old and New Testaments are authoritative for Christian faith and practice. The scriptures contain extensive teaching beyond the basic and decisive gospel message. When people come to believe the foundational message about Jesus Christ and decide to follow the Christian way, they commit themselves to listen to the scriptures' detailed instructions about how to believe and live as a Christian. In other words, in their decision to become Christians they place themselves under the authority of the scriptures. The authority of the Holy Scripture is a doctrine of faith and makes sense only from an insider perspective.

But things look different from an outsider's perspective. If you have not yet come to believe the gospel of Jesus Christ, you have not yet placed yourself under the authority of the scriptures. In other words, as an outsider you don't feel an obligation to conform to Scripture simply because of its authority. It is important to keep the two perspectives distinct. In my view, we should not urge nonbelievers to accept the Christian faith simply because of the authority of Scripture. We cannot expect them to view the scriptures from an insider angle before they come to faith. Additionally, this strategy would require the apologist to offer evidence for the authority and inspiration of the scriptures and defend them from attacks apart from a decision about the gospel message of Jesus Christ. Such an approach would lead to interminable debates and would delay the decision about Jesus indefinitely. The proper order is to confront the basic message about Jesus Christ as witnessed to by the reports recorded in the New Testament writings, examine them as one would examine other historical claims and make a decision to believe or not. If we come to faith in Jesus Christ through the testimony of the apostles, then we will acknowledge the unique placement of those who witnessed these events. We will gladly put ourselves under their authority as our teachers to whom we look for detailed instruction in Christian faith and life.

What is the gospel? What is the fundamental and decisive message about which one must decide in order to transition from not possessing Christian faith to possessing it? For the Apostles, the core of the Christian message is that Jesus Christ is Lord and Christ, and they offered as evidence for that assertion their witness to resurrection of Jesus from the dead. As we continue, I hope to clarify the meaning of this claim and present evidence that puts us in a position to make a rational and responsible decision to embrace this faith.

20

MOVING INTO FAITH—RATIONAL AND RESPONSIBLE?

In the last two chapters I clarified the idea of history, located the source of information decisive to the transition from nonbelief into Christian faith and clarified the distinction between outsider and insider views of this source. Now let's imagine an outsider's actual encounter with the core Christian message and specify the judgment demanded in this situation.

Moving from nonbelief into Christian belief requires us to believe reports of events to which we have no direct access on the word of those who claim to have had direct access. This encounter is exceedingly complex, way beyond our ability to describe fully. The following are some general categories that affect the outcome of this encounter: (1) the background beliefs, experiences, questions and interests of the nonbeliever; (2) the relationship between the witnesses reporting the events and the nonbeliever listening to the story; (3) the nature of the events reported; and (4) the perceived advantages or disadvantages of accepting the report. Obviously, we cannot create a description of the event of hearing and believing the gospel that anticipates the details of every encounter.

Perhaps some analogies will help. Suppose I am visiting an unfamiliar city and need a prescription filled. I ask the hotel concierge for directions to the local Walgreens. I listen to the directions carefully, accept them fully without consciously examining them critically and follow them trustingly. Or in another analogy, when I was a child my father told me that he served in United States Navy in the Pacific during World War II. I believed him immediately and without reservation. Or again, suppose that shortly after I return home from work my neighbor rings my door bell and warns me that in my absence today she saw an unfamiliar man step into my yard and peer into my dining room window. Will I believe her or not? Will I take appropriate measures in response to my belief that these events happened? In one final analogy, suppose a stranger approaches me on a street corner as I wait for the "Walk" sign to illuminate. He tells the story of how a few years ago on a hike in the Santa Monica Mountains he spotted a group of men burying piles of cash. Sadly, they placed a huge rock over the spot so big that he could not move it. After returning from his hike the stranger drew a map to the hidden treasure, which he will happily sell to me for $100. The sign across the street flashes "Walk." I continue on my way without any reservations about having walked away from the buried treasure and a secure retirement.

In each of these four analogies we can see at work the four general factors mentioned above. I bring to each of these encounters the whole package of my beliefs and expectations, I have some kind of relationship to the witness, the events presented for belief possess a certain character and I have a feel for the cost of believing or not believing the reports. Each of these factors plays a part in my decision. Most of the time, we are not even aware of the processes by which we perceive and weigh these factors and come to believe.

At this point I want to return to an idea I discussed in the first few chapters, applying it in the present context. I believe there is more to the belief-forming process than perceiving and weighing evidences. In much modern thought about belief formation, it is presumed that being a responsible and rational person requires us to consider doubt as the initial attitude toward testimony. Only the *measurable* weight of testimony, the *demonstrable* credibility of the witnesses and other *articulable* evidences can propel the mind from its initial doubt into belief. I object to this account of the transition from not believing to believing for two reasons. First, as my analogies show, in many cases we are able to evaluate the complex factors in a rational decision to believe very rapidly. We need not and cannot articulate a detailed assessment of our processing of these factors. Attempting to do so would be as foolish as impossible. Only neurotics spend enormous amounts of time and energy attempting to articulate and weigh every factor in their decisions. To live we must take risks. There is a second reason I object to the modern preference for doubt. I think it is more descriptive of what we actually do to assume that we possess a natural tendency to believe unless there is a reason not to believe. In other words, our first inclination is to believe what other people tell us rather than doubt them. We do not have an obligation as rational persons to doubt what others say unless there is a reason to doubt.

Getting clear that we do not have an obligation to begin with doubt will help us clear our minds of unreasonable rules that bias us against the testimony of the apostles before we hear it. It will allow us to listen to the witnesses' stories with openness to being persuaded. The four factors for belief formation will still play their part but without the extra burden of a false description of what it means to be a rational person. Of course, as my example of the treasure map shows, we can sometimes have good reasons to doubt what people say. But simply that we are being asked to trust the word of another person is not good reason to doubt.

21

THE RESURRECTION OF JESUS: THE EVENT THAT CHANGES EVERYTHING

In this chapter we finally get to the decisive event in Christian history, the resurrection of Jesus of Nazareth. If this event really happened as the first Christians believed, everything changes. If they were wrong and it did not happen, Christianity as it originally came to exist and developed through the centuries is false. In the next few chapters, we will pursue the question of whether or not we can reasonably hold to the resurrection faith.

We hear the Christian message from within our wider and narrower contexts. We bring our own beliefs, thoughts, experiences and expectations to this encounter. In this book we are asking how a contemporary person can make a rational judgment and responsible decision to believe the Christian message. I think a good place to begin is to reflect on how the very first Christians made their transition into Christian faith. Surely, our coming to responsible faith cannot be wholly different from theirs.

Our knowledge of the careers of the first Christians comes from the documents of the New Testament, especially from the Four Gospels, Acts and the letters of Paul. Let's delay the question of the historical reliability of these sources and concentrate on the story. The first Christians were Jews and came from among the original disciples of Jesus. They believed in the God of Israel and looked to the

Law and the Prophets for guidance in their religion and life. After Jesus began to preach about the coming kingdom of God, these people and many others flocked to hear his message and witness his actions. Because of his radical teaching, bold actions and the miracles he performed, people speculated about who he was and how to fit him into their categories. Was he a prophet? Was he the Messiah-King? Was he an apocalyptic fanatic? They speculated about his aims. Did he aim to liberate the Jews from Roman rule? Did he intend to bring the age to an end with divine judgment and renewal? Jesus did not fit in any preconceived category.

Jesus called twelve of his disciples into his inner circle, but there was also a larger circle of above a hundred close disciples. Apparently, even these intimate disciples were not much clearer than others about who Jesus was and what his intentions were. But they were loyal to Jesus and were certain that the God of Israel was doing something new in the person and ministry of Jesus. According to the Gospel of Mark, Peter came to believe that Jesus was "the Messiah" (8:29). But it's hard to tell exactly what Peter meant by the title.

When Jesus arrived at Jerusalem, debated with the Pharisees, entered the Temple and drove out the money changers, the religious and political leaders of Jerusalem were alarmed. They captured Jesus, tried him at night and convinced the Roman governor Pilate to crucify him. Jesus was crucified in the presence of solders, enemies, the curious crowd and his friends. His disciples saw him die. Some of them were able to secure his body and bury it in a nearby tomb.

What must his disciples have thought about this end to the story? Did God abandon Jesus? Was Jesus self-deceived? Or did Jesus simply suffer a martyr's death as did many of the ancient prophets? According the gospel accounts, the disciples were stunned, afraid and disappointed. But then something happened they did not expect. On Sunday morning, less than 48 hours after they had seen Jesus die and be buried, some women visited the tomb where Jesus had been buried and found it open and empty. Peter ran to the tomb to see for himself, and seeing the empty tomb, he wondered what had happened (Luke 24:12). Shortly thereafter, Jesus appeared to Peter and the other disciples and spoke with them. Contrary to all expectations, Jesus had been raised from the dead. This experience of the risen Jesus changed everything. Everything had to be rethought and reoriented.

The writings of Paul are the earliest preserved witness by someone who experienced a resurrection appearance. According to his own words, Paul persecuted the first Christians but was confronted by Jesus himself and called to preach the gospel—a most unlikely convert! In Acts, we have three extensive accounts of the conversion of Saul. But I am concentrating here on Paul's words from his own pen. In 1 Corinthians 15, Paul bases his central argument for the general, end-time resurrection of the dead on the complete consensus of the first Christians that Jesus was raised from the dead: to deny the general resurrection is to deny the resurrection of Christ. But that Christ arose from the dead was a foundational belief in Corinth and all other churches. Paul lists those to whom Jesus appeared after his resurrection: Peter, the Twelve, James, the 500 (many of who were still alive), all the apostles, and finally Jesus appeared to Paul himself. According to Galatians 1:18-20, Paul spent two weeks with Peter in Jerusalem and while there visited with James the Lord's brother. Hence we have in the words of Paul a direct witness from one who saw the resurrected Lord. Not only so, Paul was personally acquainted with many others who also independently saw the risen Jesus.

Two conclusions follow from these considerations: (1) there can be no doubt that the event that caused the disciples to believe that God raised the crucified Jesus from the dead marks the decisive beginning of Christianity. Without it, Christianity would not exist. Christian faith is more than belief in the resurrection, but belief in the resurrection is essential and it changes dramatically how the teachings, miracles and the death of Jesus must be understood. (2) There can be no doubt that Paul, Peter, James the Lord's brother, the twelve and many others experienced an appearance of Jesus, which for them unambiguously demonstrated that Jesus had been raised from the dead. Many questions remain for us to address, but I think these conclusions are sound historical judgments.

22

THE RESURRECTION OF JESUS: WHAT IT MEANS

In the previous chapter, I described the earliest witnesses' testimony about the resurrection of Jesus. I argued from this testimony to two conclusions: belief in the resurrection of Jesus stands at the very origin of Christianity. Belief that God raised Jesus Christ from the dead is the lens through which the original disciples interpreted all their previous experience with Jesus. Apart from this faith, Christianity would not exist. Additionally, we can conclude that Paul, Jesus' closest associates, and many others really experienced appearances they believed to be the resurrected Jesus.

I want to delay addressing the question about the truth of the resurrection faith, that is, the question "Did Jesus really rise from the dead?" We need to deal with another issue first: what did it mean to the first witnesses that shortly after his death and burial Jesus' tomb was found empty and that he appeared to them alive? Christianity is not built on the brute fact of the resurrection miracle. The resurrection faith is a belief about an event within the flow of history, and historical events manifest their meaning in relation to their immediate and remote historical contexts. As we read Paul, Acts and other New Testament writings, we see the far-reaching significance the first Christians perceived in the event of the resurrection of Jesus.

What is the historical context that gives the resurrection its significance? I have to oversimplify matters a bit, but I think the most important aspects of that context are: (1) the life of Jesus as experienced and remembered by his disciples; (2) contemporary speculations, beliefs and hopes surrounding death and resurrection and beliefs about God's historical plan for defeating evil and saving his people; and (3) the impact of the resurrection appearances themselves.

Clearly, it matters who died, whose tomb was found empty, who appeared alive and to whom. Apart from a few references in the New Testament letters, Acts, Revelation and Hebrews, we know the disciples' experiences and remembrances of Jesus from the Four Gospels. Without going into great detail, let's consider how they remembered Jesus, limiting ourselves to the Gospel of Mark. Jesus entered the public eye when he began preaching "The kingdom of God is near. Repent and believe the good news" (Mk 1:15). He calls disciples to become "fishers of men" (Mk. 1:17). He exorcises demons from the possessed, and the demons recognize him as "the Holy One of God" (1:24). Jesus heals a leper (1:40-45). When he healed a paralytic man, Jesus accompanies his healing command with "Son, your sins are forgiven" (2:5). He declared himself "Lord of the Sabbath" (2:28). Jesus calms the storm on the Sea of Galilee with the words "Quiet, be still" (4:39). A woman received healing at the touch of his robe (5:29), and a little girl was raised back to life from death when Jesus said, "Little girl, I say to you, get up" (5:41). He healed the deaf and the blind and fed 5,000 and 4,000 in the desert. He takes Peter, James and John up to a secluded place on a mountain and is transfigured before them (9:2-13).

Jesus spoke with personal authority unlike any rabbi or prophet ever spoke. As we saw above, in dealing with the demons and with death and disease, he spoke in his own name. We can see this also in the Gospel of Matthew in the Sermon on the Mount. Jesus says that you have heard it said but "I say to you" (Mt 5:39, 44). And at the end of that sermon, the crowds were amazed because "he taught as one who had authority, and not as the teachers of the law" (Mt 7:28-29).

Jesus performed symbolic actions that pronounced judgment on the ruling powers. He rode into Jerusalem on donkey in triumphal procession. He cursed the fig tree for bearing no fruit and entered the Temple and drove out the money changers. In Mark 13, Jesus speaks of the coming Judgment on the City of Jerusalem and identifies himself ("the Son of Man") as the judge who will bring this judgment (13:26-27). And on the night he was betrayed, Jesus celebrated the Passover with his disciples. During this memorial of God's great act of salvation from Egypt, Jesus did something amazing. He changed the meaning of Passover ceremony. As he shared the bread and wine of the Passover, he said, "This is my body" and "This is the blood of the New Covenant which is poured out for many" (Mk 14:22-25). In this act, Jesus claimed that his impending death would bring about a new deliverance and a new covenant.

That night Judas betrayed Jesus, and Peter denied him three times. And at his trial before the Sanhedrin, the High Priest asked Jesus, "Are you the Christ, the Son of the Blessed One" (Mk 14:61). Jesus answered unambiguously, "I am. And you will see the Son of Man sitting on the right hand of the Mighty One and coming on the clouds of heaven" (14:62). The next morning Jesus was executed by the Romans on a cross as a blasphemer and a rebel. Joseph of Arimathea, a "prominent member of the Council" asked Pilate to release the body of Jesus. Joseph placed Jesus' body in a tomb cut out of rock. Mary Magdalene and Mary the mother of Joses "saw where he was laid" (15:47).

Now we have before us the first aspect of the historical context that determines the meaning of the resurrection of Jesus. It was *Jesus* who was resurrected, the person the disciples knew intimately. We will say more about this later, but even now we can see that the resurrection of Jesus would have validated and made clear the significance of his amazing teaching, claims and deeds.

23

"WHO IS THIS?" THE RESURRECTION OF JESUS AS THE ANSWER

We continue now with the theme of the meaning of the resurrection of Jesus Christ. As I said previously, the meaning of an historical event is determined by its surrounding circumstances. To understand the impact of the resurrection faith on the disciples and their interpretation of its meaning, we need to set the resurrection event into three contexts: (1) the life of Jesus as experienced and remembered by his disciples; (2) contemporary speculations, beliefs and hopes surrounding death and resurrection and beliefs about God's historical plan for defeating evil and saving his people; and (3) the impact of the resurrection appearances themselves.

In the preceding chapter we dealt with the first context, the life of Jesus. We saw that Jesus was remembered as an extraordinary figure, as performing miracles, forgiving sins, speaking with authority, exhibiting unheard of familiarity and intimacy with God and making claims about himself that struck his adversaries as blasphemous. These extraordinary acts and claims left everyone asking, "Who is this?" This question voices their sense of not having a category into which Jesus easily fit. Something new is happening. But then he was crucified by the Romans at the instigation of the religious leaders of the Jews for blasphemy and rebellion. The judgment and execution of Jesus as a blasphemer and a rebel contradicted the entire trajectory of Jesus' life and teaching and negated the expectations that had arisen in the hearts of those who knew him best and loved him most.

The question, "Who is this?" seemed to have been answered: *not what we had hoped*. But the resurrection placed the question "Who is this?" on a completely different plane. Not only must the disciples ask, "Who is this who raises the dead, speaks with authority, opens the eyes of the blind, makes the lame walk and forgives sins?" The resurrection forced the addition, "and who was crucified as a blasphemer and rebel but whom God raised from the dead?" Who is *this?*

The second context within which we must interpret the resurrection faith is "the contemporary speculations, beliefs, and hopes surrounding death and resurrection and beliefs about God's historical plan for defeating evil and saving his people." When the first disciples concluded from the resurrection appearances and the discovery of the empty tomb that Jesus had been raised from the dead, what did they think about its significance? The most important data relevant to this question come from the New Testament itself. There are also relevant data in documents contemporary with the New Testament, but we must be cautious about generalizations. Historians who study this era point out that there is no one "Jewish" view of resurrection and eternal life. Some did not believe in the resurrection or in any form of life beyond death and others may have believed in the survival of the spirit at the death of the body. We see in the New Testament itself that not everyone believed in resurrection; the Sadducees did not. But the Pharisees believed that God would bring about a future age in which the righteous dead would be raised bodily to everlasting life. For the Pharisees, the resurrection of the dead signaled the end of the age of death and the abolition of sin, disease, violence and oppression and the dawning of a new age.

Jesus' teaching on the resurrection was clearly nearer to the Pharisees than to the Sadducees. He argued for the resurrection, claiming that the Sadducees do not understand Scripture and don't know the power of God (Matt 22:23-32). If you follow Jesus in this age, enduring the suffering that accompanies discipleship, you will be rewarded "in the resurrection of the righteous" (Luke 14:4). Paul argues with those in Corinth who do not believe in the resurrection of the dead (1 Cor 15). He refutes crude caricatures that view the resurrection as restoration of our present corruptible bodies. Nevertheless, he argues for a bodily resurrection at the end of the age. The resurrection overcomes death, transforms the corruptible and mortal body into an incorruptible and immortal body. Paul clearly affirms the resurrection of the body, not merely the survival of the spirit. But the resurrection of the body is also a radical transformation of the body. For Paul, resurrection means restoration of life in continuity with the identity, history and bodily existence that otherwise would be destroyed forever by physical death. Also, like the Pharisees, Paul sees the resurrection as signaling the end of the age and the definitive transformation of the world.

Set in this context it stands out clearly that Paul and the rest of the New Testament view the "resurrection" of Jesus as the restoration of his life and transformation of his physical body into a mode of life expected only at the end of the age, namely incorruptibility and immortality. The notion that Paul (or any other New Testament witness) could have conceived of Jesus' "resurrection" merely as the survival his spirit or justness of his cause, is highly implausible.

Now we have another piece of the puzzle to help us understand the meaning of Jesus' resurrection. The early disciples, the first Christians, understood Jesus' resurrection as an "end time" event. He was saved from death by God through the restoration of his life and transformation of the body in which he had been born, performed his works and died on a cross.

"Who is this?" He is the beginning of the resurrection of the dead, the end of the age of sin and death and the beginning of the new age of eternal life. Through his resurrection Jesus' universal significance is revealed, for the resurrection of the dead is about the destiny of the whole world, all time and space and everyone. And because his resurrection possesses universal significance, so do his death, his teaching, his acts and his birth.

24

THE DAMASCUS ROAD REVELATION AND PAUL'S GOSPEL

We have been pursuing the idea that the event of the resurrection of Jesus, set in its historical context of the acts, teaching and death of Jesus, contemporary ideas about the resurrection of the dead at the end of the age and the resurrection appearances themselves, contains the core gospel at the origin of Christianity. In this chapter we will consider some New Testament texts that refer to the resurrection appearances. Since in this section so far we are not presupposing Christianity's truth but examining the evidence for this conclusion, I will proceed with some historical caution. Hence I will give the highest priority to testimony from sources historians consider as having the most direct access to the appearances of the resurrected Jesus.

All New Testament writings presuppose or explicitly refer to the resurrection of Jesus. The Four Gospels narrate Jesus' appearances to his original disciples, the women who visited the tomb, Peter, John and the others. The Book of Acts presents the preaching and testimony of Peter and Paul concerning the resurrection. A good case can be made that these accounts derive from the people who actually experienced the appearances first hand. But Paul's direct testimony is recorded in his own words in letters written by him. Someone might argue that the narrations in the Gospels or Acts or Hebrews are indirect, second or third-hand, and therefore could differ from the original witnesses' testimony. No such argument can be made about Paul's testimony in 1 Thessalonians, 1 & 2 Corinthians, Romans and Philippians. In this case, we must choose to believe Paul or not believe him. There is no issue of corruption in transmission.

Paul teaches about the significance of the resurrection of Jesus in many places (For example, Phil 3:10-11, 20-21; 1 Thess 1:9b-10; 4:13-18; Rom 1:1-4; 4:18-25; 6:1-10; 8:9-11, 22-26; 10:9-10; 14:7-9; and 2 Cor 4:7-15). But he refers to his own experience of the risen Jesus three times, twice in 1 Corinthians and once in Galatians:

> "Am I not free? Am I not an apostle? Have I not seen Jesus our Lord? Are you not the result of my work in the Lord?" (1 Cor 9:1).

> "For what I received I passed on to you as of first importance: that Christ died for our sins according to the Scriptures, [4] that he was buried, that he was raised on the third day according to the Scriptures, [5] and that he appeared to Cephas, and then to the Twelve. [6] After that, he appeared to more than five hundred of the brothers and sisters at the same time, most of whom are still living, though some have fallen asleep. [7] Then he appeared to James, then to all the apostles, [8] and last of all he appeared to me also, as to one abnormally born" (1 Cor 15:3-8).

> "I want you to know, brothers and sisters, that the gospel I preached is not of human origin. [12] I did not receive it from any man, nor was I taught it; rather, I received it by revelation from Jesus Christ. [13] For you have heard of my previous way of life in Judaism, how intensely I persecuted the church of God and tried to destroy it. [14] I was advancing in Judaism beyond many

> of my own age among my people and was extremely zealous for the traditions of my fathers. [15] But when God, who set me apart from my mother's womb and called me by his grace, was pleased [16] to reveal his Son in me so that I might preach him among the Gentiles, my immediate response was not to consult any human being. [17] I did not go up to Jerusalem to see those who were apostles before I was, but I went into Arabia. Later I returned to Damascus" (Gal 1:11-17).

The topic we are considering is so huge that many books could be written on it. Sadly, I have time and space to make only one point. The two references to "revelation" in Galatians 1:11-17 (quoted above), considered along with the other two texts from Paul quoted above, clearly refer to the appearance of the resurrected Christ to Paul (cf. Acts 9, 22, and 24). In verse 12, Paul says he received his gospel by revelation. In verses 13-16, he elaborates on this revelation, its context and its results. Before this revelation, Paul thought he should persecute the church and be zealous for the traditions of his fathers. But God intervened and graciously revealed "his Son in me." Paul's experience of the resurrected Jesus as divine grace and as God's choice to have mercy on a sinner and an enemy (cf. Rom 5:1), definitively shaped his understanding of the gospel. The good news proclaims that God's grace and mercy do not depend on our works of righteousness. And, if we don't have to win God's grace and avoid God's wrath by scrupulously keeping the Law, God's people can be opened to the Gentiles by faith in Jesus!

Further elaboration of the meaning and implications of the resurrection would lead us deep into the field of Christology. My point so far in this section on the resurrection is to show that the resurrection is not merely a brute fact, a miracle whose meaning is exhausted by its unusual nature. Given its context in the life of Jesus, the religious thought of the day and in the lives of those to whom the resurrected Jesus appeared, we can see how Jesus' resurrection implied a religious revolution that has in fact changed the world.

25

THE CASE FOR THE RESURRECTION: SOME ADVICE FOR APOLOGISTS

We begin now to address the question of the historical facticity of the resurrection of Jesus, which, as I have emphasized, is the crucial event at the origin of Christianity. All subsequent Christian history and teaching is premised on the reality of the resurrection. As Paul readily admits, "if Christ is not risen" (1 Cor 15:14-19), the Christian message is false, the Christian way of life is useless and the Christian hope is groundless. It has taken us four chapters on the resurrection to get to this point. We had to get a feel for how the first believers understood the event of the resurrection. How else could we know what is at stake in our decision to accept or reject their witness? Now we know that to believe that Jesus was raised from the dead is to accept a radical reorientation in our worldview and a revolution in our way of life. Likewise, to reject the bodily resurrection of Jesus is to reject all that flows from it, the forgiveness of sins, hope of the resurrection, the identity of God, the meaningfulness of suffering and the love of God.

Allow me to remind readers that are now dealing with the fourth decision point on the journey from atheistic materialism to full Christian faith. In my opinion, only those who have gone through the first three decision points are ready to face the question of the historical facticity of the resurrection of Jesus. What sense does it make to present a case for the resurrection of Jesus to a materialist? Nor is a polytheist or pantheist or committed deist ready to make a rational judgment or a responsible decision about it. If the atheist or deist could have seen the crucifixion and burial of Jesus on Good Friday and accompanied the women to the tomb on Sunday morning to see the empty tomb and meet Jesus alive, or if they had been struck down like Paul on the Damascus Road and heard Jesus speak directly to them, perhaps they would have come to believe in Jesus' resurrection and existence of God *at the same time.* Perhaps they would not deny the evidence gathered by their own eyes and ears. But we cannot reproduce these events for them. We have only the testimony of those who say they experienced them and the testimony of those who first believed them.

For those who do not want to believe in the resurrection of Jesus, there are plenty of ways to evade this conclusion. If you are an atheist, you think you know apart from any historical evidence that the resurrection did not happen, because, since there is no God, God could not have raised Jesus. No evidence will move you. Deists respond much the same way. God set up the world to run on its own and does not interfere. Since God never interferes with course of natural events, God did not reverse the course of nature in Jesus' case either. If atheists or deists bother with history at all, they see their job as finding plausible naturalistic explanations for historical reports of miracles. They speculate that the supposed eye and ear witnesses were mistaken or they lied. The reports do not come from eye witnesses but from hearsay, and whatever really happened, the story has become overlain with legend or myth.

For those who believe in the one God who made the world and sustains it in existence every moment, for those who are open to divine revelation in nature and history and for those who have no rational or theological objections to miracles, denials that are based on presupposed atheism or deism don't carry much weight. They are either irrelevant because they presuppose atheism when we are convinced of God's existence or they are disingenuous because they make metaphysical objections in the guise of historical arguments.

My reading of Christian apologetic literature leads me to conclude that many of these works do not take the preceding cautions into account and make other serious mistakes that limit their value in helping people come to faith: (1) they do not take care to follow the most rational decision cascade from atheism to full Christian faith; (2) they fall into the evidentialist trap of accepting the burden of proof; (3) they give the impression of anxiety, of being over-eager to convince; or (4) they overstate their case, providing easy targets for rebuttal. Each of these mistakes in its own way deflects nonbelievers' attention away from the seriousness of their situation and from the necessity of making a decision in the moment.

Perhaps these considerations will help you understand why I am somewhat impatient with objections to the resurrection faith that are based on atheism, deism or any other philosophy that denies the possibility of miracles. Responding to such objections is fruitless endeavor. I am also impatient with equivocations, demands for more evidence and alternative ways of explaining the resurrection faith that seem to be designed to evade the real issue. The division between faith and unbelief is not merely a matter of dispassionately weighing evidence in some neutral scales. It is also a matter of friendship or hostility, of love or hate; hence, this decision has an unmistakable moral dimension. Paul and the others claim they know that Jesus Christ was raised from the dead, and they staked the meaning of their entire existence on this fact. Either they are correct or they are lying or they are mistaken. You have to look them in the eyes and say, "I believe you" or "I don't believe you." You have to make a decision and live with it. And you have to do it now. This is a vital component of any apologetic situation. Any apologetic that does not make this clear risks failure.

26

JESUS IS RISEN—HISTORY'S PROBABILITY AND LOVE'S CERTAINTY!

It is a huge mistake to think of the question of the resurrection of Christ merely as a philosophical or historical problem. Approaching it as if it could be limited in this way will lead to interminable debates and wild speculation. In this chapter I want to place the question of the resurrection into a larger framework that better models how a person actually comes to believe reasonably and responsibly

First, of course philosophical reason and historical methods play a role. Christianity does not ask us to believe contradictions or impossibilities. Nor does it ask us to believe that an event happened that we know did not happen. We've already looked at some of New Testament statements about the resurrection from a historical perspective. Paul's testimony in 1 Corinthians and Galatians possesses the strongest historical warrant in the New Testament because it is direct, firsthand. The number of ways we can respond to Paul's claim is limited. We can believe that he is telling the truth about his experience and interpreting it correctly or that he is lying or mistaken. Paul also tells us in his own words that Jesus appeared alive after his death and burial to Peter, James, John and many others (1 Cor 15). We know that a few years after his conversion—more than three but not more than 5 or 6—Paul met Peter and James the Lord's brother in person. He stayed 15 days with Peter (Gal 1:18-19). Hence Paul was in a position to hear about Peter's and James' (and others') encounters with the resurrected Jesus from their own mouths. We must either believe or disbelieve Paul's claim to have met with Peter and James, and through Paul we are placed in the position of having to believe or disbelieve Peter's and James' testimony about the resurrection.

Now add to this most direct historical connection, the accounts in Acts and the Four Gospels. (I place them second in historical weight because we can't say how much is direct and how much is indirect testimony.) In Acts, we have accounts of Peter's and Paul's preaching and Paul's Damascus Road experience. In the Gospels, we have very detailed accounts of the crucifixion, and we hear the story of Jesus' burial, the empty tomb and some resurrection appearances. The facts mentioned in Acts and the Gospels are also supported in Paul, including the empty tomb, the dramatic conversion of Paul, the appearances to Peter and the others. Hence we have a historical warrant to fill in the gaps in Paul's testimony by using Acts and the Gospels.

There is no doubt that if we possessed this level of historical support for an "ordinary" historical event, no one would doubt that it really happened. Supposed we substitute for Paul's claim to have seen Jesus Christ alive, the claim of having visiting the Temple in Jerusalem after his visit to Arabia. Suppose further that this fact is mentioned in the Four Gospels and Acts and serves as an assumption for the rest of the New Testament documents. No historian would doubt it. Indeed no historian would even think of doubting it. It would be historically certain. But because it is a *miracle,* a miracle with revolutionary, world historical, religious, moral and metaphysical significance, some people are willing to entertain the most outlandish conspiracy theories and speculative alternatives to the resurrection. Paul, the Pharisee and persecutor of Christians, changed from persecutor to persecuted preacher because of a deception? Peter, James the Lord's brother and all the rest conspired to deceive the world? The disciples saw Jesus die but lost track of his body after his death? Historically speaking—leaving out the bias against miracles and the epic implications of the resurrection—any event as directly and widely document as the resurrection of Jesus would be accepted as historically established without question. Hence no one can be warranted *historically* for rejecting the resurrection. There must be another reason.

Second, to think reasonably about the resurrection event in historical terms, one cannot apply the presupposition that miracles cannot happen. To do so would make historical argument a waste of time. In the previous chapter I argued that believers should not take seriously historical objections to the resurrection based on atheism or deism. The discussion must be focused elsewhere, that is, on one of the first three decision points in the move from atheism to full Christian faith.

Third, belief in the event of the resurrection *from a historical perspective* is just like belief in any other event. But from an existential, moral and religious perspective, belief in the resurrection is dramatically different. Belief in the resurrection of Jesus Christ demands from us what it demanded from Paul and the first disciples, a complete change of life direction! To say believingly "Jesus is risen!" is to say "Jesus is my Teacher, my Lord and my Savior." It is to reject ordinary, prudential, worldly life and risk everything! From this perspective, to believe Paul, Peter, James the Lord's brother, the women at the tomb and all the rest appears as a very scary proposition. Even if historical science tells us that the resurrection really happened and even if rejecting the resurrection requires us to consider outlandish conspiracy theories, we still hesitate.

At this point in the argument, apologists often attempt to construct an argument for the trustworthiness of the New Testament witnesses, centering perhaps on the fact that they gave their lives for their testimony. And I have no strong objection to these arguments. But these arguments create incentives to rebut and think of reasons to doubt. Arguments always create their dialectical opposites. Hence I want to take another approach. In his *Confessions,* book 10, Augustine of Hippo expresses confidence that his readers will believe him when they read his confessions to God, which they cannot check out for themselves, because their "ears are opened by love." He says, with reference with 1 Corinthians 13:7 "love believes all things, at least among those love has bonded to itself and made one." In his reflections on faith, Gabriel Marcel speaks of the certainty of faith as an intersubjective bond that not only credits but "rallies to" the one in whom it believes *(The Mystery of Being,* Vol. 2). The certainty of faith in the resurrection arises when we get to know the New Testament witnesses, enter into their minds and hearts and see through their eyes. In other words, we believe them because we love them. If we don't love them, we will not believe them.

Fourth, how can we get over the scariness of the revolution called for by the resurrection faith? Augustine famously said, "For my part, I should not believe the gospel except as moved by the authority of the Catholic Church." Believing in the resurrection is not merely a matter of examining the credibility of some 2,000 year old documents. You have to love the people who bore and bear witness to Jesus. You have to see that the resurrection faith and all that flows from it produces good people, people whose virtue and love you admire. The church should be, and sometimes actually is, the living reality that embodies the revolution implied in the resurrection of Jesus. How can a nonbeliever, one who understands practically nothing about the New Testament, come to love Jesus and those who loved him first, that is, Paul, Peter, and the others? Only if they get to know a living human being who loves Jesus, Paul, Peter and the others! Only if they are loved by someone who has been transformed by their faith and love for Jesus, Paul, Peter and the others! The church—I mean the living body of believers under Christ their head—helps people believe by helping them love, and it helps them to love by loving them.

27

"THIS I KNOW, FOR THE BIBLE TELLS ME SO"

We have come to the point in our discussion of the resurrection of Jesus where we can see clearly what is involved in a reasonable and responsible decision to believe and adopt the Christian faith and life. If we've studied the first disciples' recorded memories of Jesus' life, teachings and death, if we've listened to the testimonies of Paul, Peter, James the Lord's brother and many others to the resurrection, if we've been favorably impressed with the way of life of the early disciples, if we know and admire some contemporary believers and if we are attracted to the Christian hope, I believe our decision to enter the Christian way can be reasonably and responsibly made. This transition is not best described as an inference from premises to conclusion or an inference to the best explanation or a decision about the level of probability that a narrated event really happened. It is certainly not a blind leap of faith or a careless fall into wishful thinking. It is best described as the deepening of a personal relationship from respectful listening to trust and love for those who are in a position to know what we do not.

As a personal relationship of trust and love, faith makes a decisive commitment. It does not deny the possibility that it could be wrong, that it could be deceived. But it will not accept an obligation to withhold commitment while it anxiously seeks more evidence to confirm its trust. Nor does faith proportion its commitment to the weight of probability on each side. Genuine trust and love pushes aside the whispering voice of doubt that says, "But what if you are wrong?" Faith asserts in response, "I understand that I cannot know absolutely that I am right, but I *believe* that I am right. And I have decided and am determined to live as if I am right, *even if I am wrong!*"

Beyond the Fourth Decision Point

We have made the decisive move beyond the fourth decision point, that is, the division between mere theism and Christian faith in God. Now what? What are the implications of this decision? The first result of this move is a dramatic change in our relationship to the apostles and other early disciples. As seekers and inquirers, we treated the apostles' writings as we would other historical documents. We gave them no advantage, no special deference, no authority above other texts. But once we come to believe that the apostles experienced Jesus' conquest of death in his resurrection, everything changes. Now we are eager to know everything they can teach us about Jesus Christ and how we can become his disciples. Because of their special relationship to Jesus, we accept them as our teachers, exclusively authoritative for what it means to believe, love and hope as Christians. As a matter of historical placement, no other teachers, no other texts can guide us. But this way of understanding the authority of the Bible may seem new to many, so I want to deal briefly with that concern.

The Bible Tells Me So?

The children's song says, "Jesus loves me! This I know, for the Bible tells me so." A wonderful thought! Comforting to adults as well as children! But this line in the song does raise a question. Do Christians hold all their Christian beliefs simply because the Bible tells them so? Should nonbelievers be urged to believe in Jesus simply because the Bible tells them so? But why should a nonbeliever feel obligated to believe what the Bible says simply because it says so? Should believers attempt first to convince nonbelievers of the Bible's divine authority and then argue from the Bible's authority to the truth of everything the Bible teaches? In my view, it would be a serious mistake to place a decision about the authority of the Bible before a decision about Jesus and the apostolic testimony to his resurrection. Such a stance presumes either a culture in which the Bible is already held in high esteem or it obligates us to argue from historical and rational evidence to the Bible's divine authority. Neither option is very promising. We no longer live in culture where we can assume that people will accept a claim just because the Bible says so. And most contemporary people view as implausible and unpersuasive arguments to the divine authority of the Bible from its historical reliability or internal coherence or its sublime teaching. Such arguments raise more questions than they answer.

As I argued above, I believe the proper basis for an individual's recognition and acceptance of the authority of the Bible is the act of faith in the apostolic testimony to Jesus' resurrection. Acceptance of the Bible's authority is implicit in this act. In future chapters I will continue to develop the implications of this thesis, attempting to place particular Christian teachings in their proper order in relation to the central Christian claim, that is, that God raised Jesus Christ from the dead.

28

MAKING SENSE OF CHRISTIANITY'S MANY TEACHINGS

Accepting the apostolic testimony to the resurrection of Jesus is the first step into Christian faith. As I emphasized previously, this is a huge leap, a revolution that changes the direction of our lives, places them on a new foundation and initiates a lifelong journey of learning and practice. However, as anyone with more than a superficial acquaintance with Christianity knows, Christianity involves more than belief in the resurrection. And the book addresses the question, "Is Christianity true?" not merely "Did Jesus Rise from the Dead?" How shall we continue our progress toward answering the more comprehensive question of Christianity's truth? Is there a logical order in which we can best assess the truth of Christianity's many teachings from this point onward?

The first rule I wish to lay down is this: in our examination of Christianity's teachings we should never think independently of our faith in the resurrection of Jesus. In some way—to be specified later—each Christian teaching needs to be related to the resurrection faith. This rule is of supreme importance. Only in this way can we root the full spectrum of Christian teaching in the thing to which we have the most direct access, that is, an historical event to which we have access by faith, a faith that is *our own act* of trust and commitment. In so far as we can see the connection between our basic act of faith in Jesus and Christianity's other teachings, their meaning, truth and relevance to life will come to light. We can embrace them and hold them with greater confidence and practice them with greater joy. They will no longer appear to us as disconnected and arbitrary teachings that we are supposed to believe because we can see that the Bible says so or because the church says the Bible says so. A set of arbitrary and disconnected beliefs cannot possibly illuminate our minds, focus our attention, transform our affections and order our lives toward the fullest experience of the Father of our Lord Jesus Christ in the power of the Holy Spirit. At best, we can hold them verbally and practice them legalistically.

From the perspective of the resurrection faith, Christianity's other teachings fall into two broad classes: (1) beliefs that are closely associated with the resurrection itself or that are clearly implied by the event of the resurrection and can be readily inferred from it. In earlier chapters I dealt in a general way with this first class of beliefs. The resurrection event took place in a context that gives it significance far beyond its status as mere miracle. I noted three components of that context: "(1) the life of Jesus as experienced and remembered by his disciples; (2) contemporary speculations, beliefs and hopes surrounding death and resurrection and beliefs about God's historical plan for defeating evil and saving his people; and (3) the impact of the resurrection appearances themselves." Included in this class of beliefs are: Jesus Christ is the Revealer of the character, identity and will of God, Jesus is the Revealer of the true human relationship to God, Jesus is Savior and Lord and Jesus is the long-expected Messiah. Furthermore, it does not take a long trail of reasoning to see that by raising Jesus from the dead, God approved and validated Jesus' moral and religious teachings as possessing divine authority and, perhaps above all, that God overturned the death sentence passed on Jesus and pronounced him innocent of the charges Jews and Gentiles urged against him. Hence the resurrection transformed the meaning of the crucifixion of Jesus from a human act of failure and judicial murder into a divine act of self-sacrifice and triumph.

(2) The second class of Christian beliefs is less obviously implied within the event of the resurrection but was nevertheless taught by the apostles. As I noted in the previous two chapters, our trust and love for the apostles leads us to believe their witness to the resurrection. In this act of faith we acknowledge our dependence on them for what we know about Jesus. We acknowledge that our relationship to them will always be as students to teachers. This relationship cannot be reversed. We want them to tell us everything they know about Jesus and every nuance of their understanding of his death and resurrection and reign as Lord. We need them to help us understand what it means to live on the basis of these truths.

We can see how some of what they teach follows readily from the resurrection event itself. We can even think along with them as they come to these realizations. These teachings fall into the first class (1) discussed above. But how some of their teachings are related to the resurrection event is less obvious. We have to study and think hard in order to grasp how their teachings make the connection. As an example of a doctrine with a less obvious connection to the resurrection, consider the teaching that Jesus preexisted his earthly life as the eternal Word through whom God created the world. And the line of development gets even more obscure when we consider doctrines that received their definitive formulation beyond the New Testament era. Perhaps, the doctrine of the Trinity is the best example from this group.

In future chapters, I will examine some of the most important teachings that lie close to the heart of Christianity. As we look at these teachings I will keep in mind the purpose of this book, which is to address the question "Is Christianity True?" I am not writing a catechism, that is, series of instructions on what the church teaches. I am asking about the truth of these teachings. Can we reasonably and responsibility accept them as true? This limit is why we must show the connection of each core Christian doctrine to the resurrection, for the resurrection is the decisive event. If a teaching follows from the resurrection, it warrants our acceptance.

29

WHAT ABOUT THE BIBLE? AN AUTOBIOGRAPHICAL REFLECTION

What about the Bible? Is the Bible true? Is it historically accurate? Is it a revelation from God? We often hear such questions in popular forums and in the media. And in almost every case we would be mistaken to take such questions seriously. The Bible's authority does not become an issue for us until we accept the testimony of the apostles to the resurrection of Jesus Christ. We do not accept the truth of the resurrection because the Bible says so. Instead, we become interested in what the Bible says about other matters when we come to faith in Jesus Christ. Now I want to look at the question of the Bible autobiographically.

Let's look at how the question of the Bible arises for a person born into a Christian family and surrounded by a Christian culture. I shall speak from my own experience. My experience of the Bible was always that of an insider. It was *our* book. Though I don't remember the word being used, it was the unquestioned *authority* for church life, morals and for knowledge of God and Jesus Christ. I loved to hear stories of the Old Testament heroes of faith and the New Testament stories about Jesus, Paul and Peter. The Bible provided texts for the preacher's sermons. My parents owned several copies of the Bible, which were displayed on the coffee table and night stands. At an early age I received my own copy of the King James Bible with my name inscribed inside. I came to understand that reading the Bible was a religious duty, a discipline that should be maintained for a lifetime. Memorizing important texts and in depth study was also encouraged. Religious education was identical with Bible education. And the most admired preachers were those reputed to have the most extensive knowledge of the Bible. William Chillingworth's (1602-1644) famous declaration that "The Bible alone is the religion of Protestants" certainly describes the religion of the church and family of my youth.

At some point, in my late teens I think, I discovered that there were outsiders whose view of the Bible differed dramatically from ours. I say "ours" because I had accepted the church's view of the Bible without question. That is what my parents taught me, it was the belief of all the good people at church and the ministers and it was reinforced by the consensus of Southern (American) culture. Ironically, my first encounters with external critics and doubters of the Bible were facilitated by teachers and books that wished to defend the church's view of the Bible. They wanted to reinforce my faith that the Bible is indeed worthy of the respect given it by the church. My teachers realized that an inherited and naïve faith in the Bible had to become a reasonable faith or it would not be able to withstand the scrutiny it was sure to receive from critics. I think their intuition in this matter was correct. An inherited faith must transition to chosen faith.

But I believe they were mistaken to attempt to demonstrate apart from faith that the Bible deserved the respect that the church had traditionally given it. It is impossible *to prove* that the Bible deserves to be treated as the sole authority for knowledge of God, morality and religion by arguing from its visible characteristics to its divine origin, historical reliability and moral superiority. The Bible is a huge book, or actually, a huge collection of 66 books. It spans many centuries and crosses many very different cultures. It recounts thousands of events for which we have no other sources and no independent way to confirm. It contains many writings for which we know neither the authors nor the century in which they were written. No matter how many of the Bible's marvelous characteristics we uncover we can never get close to proving that the Bible deserves the respect given it by the church. And the unhappy by-product of this effort to prove the Bible is creating doubt in the hearts of the very people these arguments are designed to help. We are courting disaster if we convince young people that they must transition from an inherited and naïve faith to a chosen and reasonable one but lead them to believe that in order to be reasonable their acceptance of the Bible's religious authority must be based on rational arguments for the Bible's perfection. Such a strategy distracts from the real decision of faith and may exile them to years of wandering in the desert of doubt and indecision.

Hence in my view, apologists for the Christian faith should resist answering directly the questions with which I began this essay: Is the Bible true? Is it historically accurate? Is it a revelation from God? Why? Because no definitive answers can be given! Any direct response will raise as many questions as it answers, and it will provoke endless counterarguments and follow-up questions. The only path forward is the one I charted in earlier chapters. We must decide—apart from any view of the authority of the Bible—whether or not to accept the apostolic testimony to Jesus' resurrection. Yours, mine and the whole church's respect for the Bible's authority rightly flows from this decision and from nowhere else. But as I hope to show in future chapters, the church's respect for the Bible has not been misplaced. It really does flow from this decision. And neither was my trust in my parents and the church of my childhood misplaced.

30

THE DECISION THAT MAKES A THOUSAND UNANSWERED QUESTIONS SUPERFLUOUS (OR AT LEAST NOT SO URGENT)

We now transition to a place from which we view this question at a very different angle. When one comes to believe and wholeheartedly embraces the apostles' testimony to the resurrection of Jesus Christ one must voice the question asked by Peter's audience on the day of Pentecost: "Brothers, what shall we do?" Theoretically, one could come to believe that God raised Jesus from the dead but retain the same way of life as before. But Peter's listeners realized that God's act of raising Jesus placed them at a crossroads of decision, because they had cooperated with their leaders in handing Jesus over to the Romans to be crucified. Peter replied to their plea, "Repent and be baptized, every one of you, in the name of Jesus Christ so that your sins may be forgiven. And you will receive the gift of the Holy Spirit" (Acts 2:38). Hence, according to Peter, coming to believe the apostolic testimony to Jesus demands a decisive act of will, that is, to repent and submit to baptism. Repentance is a change of mind and direction in life. It renounces the past and turns toward a new way of life. In submitting to baptism we admit that we cannot wash away our guilt by ourselves. Only God can forgive sins. In baptism in Jesus' name we submit to God and trust him to wash away our sins. Just as water washes away dirt from the body, the Holy

Spirit washes away guilt from the soul. In baptism we see three actors, a repentant sinner asks for the washing, the baptizer (or the church), who represents Jesus, and the Spirit. In baptism, the Spirit comes to stay and empowers the life that flows out of faith, repentance and baptism. Apart from the grace of the Holy Spirit, repentance is just a fickle human resolution and baptism is just a bath. But because of the grace of the Spirit we can mark the event of our baptism as the beginning of a new life. And that new life is accompanied by a new community and a new ethics. Consider the description of the new community that resulted from Pentecost:

> They devoted themselves to the apostles' teaching and to fellowship, to the breaking of bread and to prayer. Everyone was filled with awe at the many wonders and signs performed by the apostles. All the believers were together and had everything in common. They sold property and possessions to give to anyone who had need. Every day they continued to meet together in the temple courts. They broke bread in their homes and ate together with glad and sincere hearts, praising God and enjoying the favor of all the people. And the Lord added to their number daily those who were being saved (Acts 2:42-47).

Though these verses do not provide a complete theology of the Christian life, they do picture the transition into a new community and a new way of life. (1) As verse 42 makes clear, this community devoted itself to learning from the apostles. What did the apostles teach them? Surely they taught them the full story of Jesus and everything Jesus taught. They taught them about the significance of Jesus' death and resurrection. (2) They devoted themselves also to fellowship or *koinonia* with fellow believers. They wanted to be together to share in this new life. Christianity is not a personal philosophy one can adopt individualistically. It is a comprehensive way of living, and hence, since human beings cannot live a full life alone, it takes shape in a community that corresponds to its vision of life. (3) They broke bread together, that is, they shared meals together that were modeled on the Last Supper of the Lord. They would have begun by breaking and sharing bread and ended by drinking the cup of wine. The meal reminded them of the new covenant in the body and blood of Jesus and of the great banquet in the coming kingdom of God. (4) They prayed. This community lives in the presence of God and relies on the love of God, the grace of Jesus and the power of the Spirit.

How does the question "Is Christianity true?" look after the transition into the community of faith though repentance and baptism? First, there is still much to learn. Those first Christians "devoted themselves to the apostles' teaching." There are many questions to ask about doctrine and ethics. Misunderstandings are common. Debates occurred and continue to occur among Christians about the proper church order, the exact nature of the atonement, predestination, the sacraments and many others. But perfect understanding is not necessary before one begins the Christian life. And second, Christians find themselves questioned by outsiders, by atheists, by adherents of other religions, by deists, by adherents of heresies, by pantheists, by critics of miracles, by doubters and skeptics and many more. We are challenged on hundreds of points concerning the historical accuracy, philosophical cogency, and ethical acceptability of the Bible's teaching. And the problem of evil is always on the lips of the outside objector. Nevertheless, since we have already accepted and wholeheartedly embraced the resurrection faith and the authority of the apostles for explaining the meaning of that faith and since we have experienced the grace of God and power of the Spirit and entered into the life of the community, we need not be disturbed by these questions and challenges as if one of these objections might destroy our faith in Jesus Christ. Since we made a reasonable judgment and a responsible decision to become Christians, we need not feel jerked around by every objection. And we are not waiting for a solution to all these problems before we can live our Christian lives with confidence.

Part Three

FROM EVIDENCES TO APOLOGETICS

Part Three marks the transition into a new phase of the argument for Christianity's truth. In the previous chapters I've presented an affirmative case for making a reasonable judgment for Christianity's truth and a responsible decision to become a Christian. Much more could be said in making this case, but now I want to deal with some misunderstandings and objections to Christianity. The positive side of the argument is often called "Christian Evidences" and defensive side is often called "Christian Apologetics" or "Defense of Christianity." The necessity of the defensive phase of the argument rests first in propensity of people to misunderstand what Christianity actually is and what it really teaches. How can we make a reasonable judgment or a responsible decision about Christianity unless we possess an accurate understanding of its teachings? Some people find certain versions of Christianity incredible or morally offensive or insufferably superficial and hence hesitate to accept them. Others adopt a form of Christianity that is defective when compared to the original form taught by Jesus and the apostles. It's questionable whether one has really rejected or accepted Christianity if the form they know is not the real thing.

The second reason for the pursuing the defensive phase of the argument arises from the barrage of objections that nonbelievers hurl against Christianity's claims. Some raise objections to the existence of God or to theism or to divine revelation. They raise the problem of evil or assert that the world needs no explanation beyond itself. Others object to the moral teachings of the Bible or they deny its historical accuracy. Some offer objections to the reliability of the apostolic witnesses to the resurrection of Jesus or they object to the very possibility of miracles. The list is endless. And even if one thinks the case I made in the first phase of the argument is very strong, one may still be disturbed and caused to doubt by the many objections that are raised. Hence I want to reply to some of the most potent objections.

31

NO, MY FRIENDS, CHRISTIANITY IS *NOT* FOR EVERYONE

We've heard it said so often that it has become utterly vacuous: "Christianity is for everyone!" "Everyone is welcome!" "Come just as you are!" That's the way it works with well-worn phrases and catchy sentences. Remove them from their original contexts that gave them precision, repeat them year after year, and they become empty vessels to be filled with meanings subtly or even dramatically different from their original import. Spoken in a culture that celebrates tolerance above virtue, that prefers feeling good to being good, and that favors image over reality, the expression, "Christianity is for everyone," will be interpreted to mean "Everyone is okay just the way they are." So, in this chapter I want to say, "No, my friends, Christianity is *not* for everyone."

Christianity is not for the proud, those who will not admit that they are weak and dependent beings, mortal and needy and empty. It's not for the unrepentant. If you intend to pursue a life of lust or greed or cruelty, if you don't think you need forgiveness or renewal, if you are well and don't need a doctor, Christianity is not for you. If you have no love for God or human beings, if you have no interest in prayer or acts of mercy, if you have no desire to worship God or serve humanity, you won't find Christianity appealing. It's not for the satisfied. If you are completely content with the world, if you have no ambition beyond physical pleasure, wealth, possessions and fame, Christianity aims too high for you. So, I say it again, "No, my friends, Christianity is *not* for everyone."

Christianity is for the weak and broken. It's for those who know they are dying and need healing, mercy and grace. Christianity is for the humble, for those who morn their sins and long for a pure heart and a clean conscience. Christianity is for those who thirst for God, for those who long for a glimpse of glory. It is for those not satisfied with what the world has to offer, for those compelled to aim higher. It's for those for whom "the good life" is not good enough and only eternal life will do. I must say it yet again, "No, my friends, Christianity is *not* for everyone."

What do these thoughts have to do with apologetics or a defense of Christianity? Much, I think, much indeed. Why should anyone be interested in a form of "Christianity" that offers nothing but bland assurances that we are fine just the way we are? How can you argue for Christianity's truth about other matters if it doesn't even tell you the truth about the human condition? Who needs a doctor that won't tell you the truth about your illness because he lacks the skill to heal you! True Christianity pierces down to the heart of the human problem: we are finite, mortal, imperfect, corrupt, ignorant, blind, selfish and unhappy beings. Christianity speaks the harsh truth about what we are, who we've become and where we stand. And the remedy it offers is just as radical as the diagnoses it makes. We need forgiving, recreating and resurrecting. We have to change, die and become new people. Who can renew and perfect the creation? Who can forgive sin and overcome its power? Who can save from the annihilation of death? Who can cleanse the conscience of its guilt and empower the will to choose the good? Who can fill the human heart with faith, hope and love? God and God alone can accomplish these things.

Christianity is not cheap like water but costly like blood. It offers not pleasant reassurances but disturbing truths. It aims not to anesthetize the conscience but cleanse it. It tells us what we know deep in our hearts: we are not okay just the way we are. No, my friends, Christianity is *not* for everyone.

32

IS CHRISTIANITY AN INVESTMENT STRATEGY OR A DECISIVE ACT?

In this chapter I want to deal with a common objection to Christian belief. It goes something like this: Let us grant that the arguments made so far in this book show that it is not irrational to believe in Jesus' resurrection and all that follows from it. Let's even grant that it has made a good case for Christian faith. Still, the evidence is not so overwhelming that it makes nonbelief irrational. There may be alternative ways to account for the same set of facts even if we can't think of one. In other words, the objective evidence for the truth of Christianity does not amount to proof and, therefore, cannot reasonably be translated into subjective certainty. But the decision to become a Christian is so radical, so comprehensive, so demanding and so life changing that no one can do this without subjective certainty. But such subjective certainty goes beyond where the evidence can take you. And common sense tells us we should proportion the level of belief to the strength of evidence.

What can we say to this objection, which I will label the "proportionality objection"? Consider how the proportionality objection treats the judgment about Christianity's truth and the decision about becoming a Christian. It assumes that the type of judgments made in mathematics and logic are ideal and ought to be the standard against which every judgment is measured. These sciences possess such clarity in their terms and lucidity in their operations that they can claim certainty for their conclusions and complete confidence for actions based on them. Other rational endeavors fall short. The type of evidence used in history, metaphysics and theology does not possess the clarity and lucidity of mathematics and hence cannot lead to the level of certainty attained in mathematics. Perhaps so. But does it follow from this fact that to be rational we must proportion belief to evidence and hence hold back from the radical, comprehensive, demanding and life changing decision to become a Christian? I do not believe so.

In investing in stocks, it makes sense to diversify. If you have $100,000 to invest, you would be wise not invest all of it in stock from one company. In this case it makes sense to proportion your belief and action to the evidence. But in other areas it is impossible to divide your loyalty and action. Some things are either/or, yes/no, or on/off. You do them or you don't. You do one or the other, but not both. You can't marry someone 98%. You can't dive into the pool 75%. You can't be a little bit pregnant. Some actions require 100% decisiveness even if the evidence provides us with only 98% confidence. When it comes to action we must take risks. Becoming a Christian is an action like getting married or diving off a diving board—only more serious! You can't be 50% Christian. Hence contrary to the proportionality objection voiced above, proportioning one's Christian commitment to the evidence would not be a rational action. It would be an irrational one, since it attempts to do the impossible. It is not reasonable to appropriate rules from one area (mathematics or investing) and apply them thoughtlessly to a different area.

On a practical level, when you try to proportion belief in Christianity to the strength of the evidence supporting it, you don't become somewhat Christian or a little bit Christian; you don't become a Christian at all. The proportionality objection applied to Christianity in effect advises that, since you cannot be 100% certain that Christianity is true, you must treat it as 100% false. And it does this because it fails to understand the difference between belief and action. A person may believe strongly or weakly or not at all that there are nonhuman intelligent beings living somewhere in our universe. As long as an idea is proposed as a mere belief, something one might discuss as a curiosity or an interesting problem, it makes sense for us to place ourselves on a quantitative scale from 0 to 100% belief. But as soon as there is a call to action, we find ourselves faced with an either/or decision. Christianity issues a call to action, and it does not allow for proportionality in our response. It's all or nothing. And we don't get not to decide.

33

THOSE ARROGANT, OBNOXIOUS CHRISTIANS!

Now we will address another common objection to Christianity. It goes something like this: "So, you think your religion is *the true religion for everyone,* that Jesus Christ is the only way to God? Other religions are false and lead nowhere? Don't you think that is a bit arrogant? Aren't those who practice other faiths just as sincere in their belief and as faithful in their religious practice as you are?" As we will see in our analysis and response, this complaint, even in this brief form, contains more than one kind of objection. And it is often combined with a long list of associated objections, such as the following: "how likely is it that you just happened to be born where and when the true religion was dominant? Wouldn't God want everyone to have access to him?" All of these objections and others like them seem to originate from the intuition that religious truth should be universally available and easily accessible. Each of these objections and the intuition that energizes it deserves analysis, but in this chapter I want to focus on the question of arrogance.

First, let's subject the arrogance objection to a little analysis. Clearly, its power is contained in associating a moral fault with a truth claim, so that asserting truth becomes an arrogant act. No one wants to think of themselves as arrogant or to be thought arrogant by others. Arrogance is an attitude of personal superiority to others.

Arrogant people see their real or imaginary characteristics as indicative of their special importance. And for a person to think she or he possesses greater worth or dignity or value than others violates our sense that all people are of equal worth. It seems as ugly as it is false.

As I noted above, the arrogance objection explicitly attempts to associate the attitude of arrogance (a moral fault) with the act of claiming that Christianity is true. It implies that an attitude of personal arrogance cannot be dissociated from the truth claim. But here it makes an obvious error. In our analysis of arrogance above we saw that arrogance is a personal attitude that draws an unwarranted moral conclusion from a person's real or imaginary characteristics or possessions. Suppose I really am very rich or brilliant or accomplished in my field. Being rich or brilliant or accomplished in a field does not necessitate personal arrogance. In themselves the statements of fact that describe someone as rich or brilliant or accomplished are either true or false; they cannot be humble or arrogant. Likewise, the statement "Christianity is true" or "Jesus Christ is the only way to God" is true or false. By itself it is not arrogant or humble. Sentences can't lie or brag or show distain. Only people can be arrogant or humble.

Let's look at the "arrogance objection" from another angle. Arrogance, as I argued above, characterizes the mood of a false judgment about one's superior worth based on one's real or imagined qualities. But when believers express the judgment that Jesus Christ is the revelation of the true God or the only way to God, they are not expressing a judgment about their superiority over others. They are not even making this judgment in reliance on their own insights into God, other religions or human nature. Their judgment is not based on a direct comparison of Christianity with other religions, which would require viewing the question from a neutral position and possessing godlike powers of discernment.

Believers' affirmation that Jesus Christ is the only way to God is a statement of faith derived from their faith in the apostolic testimony to Jesus' resurrection and glorification. If God raised Jesus from the dead, Jesus is Lord and Messiah (Acts 2:36). Paul and the original apostles declare that God raised Jesus from the dead. Either they are correct or they are incorrect. Either they are lying or they are telling the truth. Contemporary Christians believe the apostles are correct when they declare "Jesus is Lord of all" (Acts 10:36). My assertion that "Jesus is Lord and Savior" is not my personal assessment attesting to my own superior judgment in matters of religion. It is my confession of faith. And when I confess Jesus' Lordship, I also confess my trust in the apostolic testimony. In their act of confessing that Jesus Christ is Lord of all, believers are not vaunting their own personal superiority over others but humbly expressing their reliance on the word of the apostles and expressing their determination to live as disciples of the Lord.

Is Jesus Lord of all? Did God raise Jesus from the dead? These questions call for "yes" or "no" answers. Arrogance has nothing to do with it.

34

"WHY HASN'T JESUS RETURNED?"

Now I want to address another set of objections to Christian belief: "If Jesus really was raised from the dead, why didn't he appear to everyone? Why didn't he remain visibly present in the world instead of ascending to heaven (Acts 1:9-11)? Why didn't the kingdom come in its fullness (Mark 9:1)? Why hasn't he returned? Why do we have to "believe" instead of "seeing?"

It seems to me that these questions arise from a sense of tension between the idea that Jesus' resurrection is of universal significance and importance and two facts: (1) that it can be known today only indirectly, that is, by believing the written word of apostles and (2) that its impact on the world is much less obvious and universal than one would expect from such an dramatic divine act.

These questions do not have to be taken as objections. They could also be serious inquiries from people of faith seeking further understanding of the significance of what they believe. But the questioner could be implying that there are no answers and that the lack of answers disproves the fact claim of the resurrection or at least that we must doubt the fact until we find satisfactory answers. Let's deal with the challenger first and then we will address the serious inquirer.

We need to take the form of these objections seriously. They don't make direct fact-denying assertions. They don't ask "How?" or "Whether?" They ask "why?" When we ask why we are asking for the purpose or end for which someone has done something. If I ask you "Why did you do that?" I could be expressing my curiosity or making an accusation of wrongdoing. If I see you digging in your back yard or climbing a ladder toward your roof or writing a letter, the question of why or to what end immediately arises in my mind. If you suddenly shove me to the ground, unless the reason for your aggression becomes immediately obvious, you won't be surprised when I ask you why you did it. The act provokes the question because we assume that people don't do things without an end in mind.

But suppose I never discover why you were climbing a ladder or why you pushed me to the ground. I do not conclude from my lack of knowledge of the purpose for your action that you didn't do it. Indeed acts are always done for purposes, but we can know that an act was done even if we do not know why the actor did it. My knowledge of a fact rests on the evidence of my having experienced it or on believing the report of someone else who experienced it. Hence knowing the purpose of an act and knowing the fact of the act can be separated. With this distinction in mind, let's return to the objections to faith with which I began.

As the New Testament recounts and reflects on the course of events after the resurrection of Jesus, it addresses the most pressing and essential questions. Why did Jesus die, and why did God raise him from the dead (See Acts 2:22-36)? Much of the theology of the New Testament is concerned to answer these questions. Of course these answers do not fully satisfy and leave us longing for deeper understanding. But the New Testament rarely addresses questions like those in our first paragraph. (2 Peter 3:3-13 is the most direct instance.) Such questions could be multiplied endlessly, for we can always speculate about why events didn't happen in a different way or didn't produce different results. Many questions about Jesus won't be answered fully until the end of history, because the event of Jesus' death and resurrection concerns the whole human situation and all of human history. But our inability to find satisfactory answers to all of our why questions about the resurrection does not defeat belief in the resurrection itself any more than my ignorance of why you climbed a ladder yesterday defeats the fact of your climb. As long we keep our focus on the testimony of Paul, Peter, James, and the rest of those to whom Jesus appeared alive after his death, we need not let our many unanswered questions rob us of assurance of the fact of the resurrection.

Despite our inability to answer definitively the "why" questions in the first paragraph, I do not believe we are forced to remain completely silent in response to them. Some speculation, even if it is finally unconvincing, may increase our confidence that there are answers to these questions, even if we don't know them. For nearly all human beings who have ever lived, God has been mysterious and hidden, unknown by clear sight or unambiguous demonstration. But God has always been somewhat knowable by faith and reason through creation and conscience. We know that we are not our own creators and lawgivers (See Rom 1:18-32). Divine hiddenness creates an opportunity for faith, free decision, moral courage and virtue—and their opposites. In Jesus Christ, God becomes a factor inside human history in a new way, as a human character in the story. Critical questions about why Jesus didn't show himself to everyone and didn't end history fail to understand that Jesus Christ didn't enter history to end it. He came, rather, to save it, redeem it and redirect it to its divinely appointed end. Even as God becomes in Christ a new factor in history, God remains hidden under the sign of the cross and in the foolishness of preaching (1 Cor 1:21). He does so for the same reason that God has always remained hidden, for the sake of faith, freedom and virtue. It would be strange to argue that God's work of salvation and redemption contradicts or undoes God's work in creation and providence. Apparently, God wants to accomplish his purpose for creation through its history and through human action. After all, creation is saved and perfected by the work of Jesus Christ whose action is both divine *and human.* And consistent with the mysterious ways of the Creator, Jesus' divine action as Lord of All is hidden in his humanity and the humanity of his people.

35

WHEN IS "EVIL" TRULY EVIL?

The problem of evil is perhaps the most popular and potent contemporary objection to belief in God. In its simplest form it goes like this: How can you believe in a good, all-powerful and all-knowing God in the face of the pain, suffering and inhumanity that plagues the world? Would a good God allow genocide on a massive scale, if he could stop it? Wouldn't an all-powerful God prevent the human death and suffering caused by tsunamis and earthquakes, if he cared? Agnostics use such questions to undermine certainty of belief in God. Atheists offer these objections as evidence against belief in the existence of God. Believers also feel the negative force of evil and sometimes feel abandoned by God and threatened by doubt.

I want to begin at the beginning and approach the subject at the most fundamental level where the question of evil first emerges. The following two questions strike me as getting about as close to the foundation as we can get: what are the conditions under which any event or series of events could be considered evil? And what quality is being attributed to an event when it is called evil?

Evil cannot exist unless something exists. Absolute nothingness is not evil or good. Whatever evil is, it exists as a quality of something else—of a thing, an event or a relation. If there were no things or events or relations, evil could not exist. Now imagine that our universe has existed eternally or that it came into existence arbitrarily and that there is no divine mind to order and direct it. Imagine further that there are no finite minds or even any living things but that the physical and chemical processes that constitute the universe will continue to operate forever, the universe evolving as it has since the Big Bang. Does evil exist in this imaginary world? Can it exist in such a world? No. Even though things are continually coming into existence and going out of existence, being built up and destroyed, no event or series of events can be considered evil. Why?

At a minimum, to designate an event or series of events as "evil" is to say that something has gone wrong. Evil is misrelation and disharmony where there should be harmony. But the concept of "going wrong" makes no sense where there is no concept of "going according to plan." And the idea of a "plan" makes no sense apart from a mind that conceives of that plan. Hence the possibility of evil depends on the existence of a real world in which the actual course of events can contradict the ideal course of events as conceived by the divine mind. If evil occurs in this real world, contradicting the divine ideal world, we can see that such evil would cause distress and disappointment in the divine being. We are not yet speaking of God the Creator in the Christian sense. We are speaking only of an all-encompassing cosmic mind.

So, what are the conditions for the emergence of the concept of evil? Something must exist and a flow of events must be taking place. There must be a plan that encompasses all things and events, and there must be a mind that contains this comprehensive plan. Only a mind can perceive the contradiction between the way things actually go and the way they are supposed to go. And only a mind that wills the good (that is, the way things are supposed to go) can experience distress when they go wrong. The concept of cosmic evil emerges only with the emergence of a cosmic mind and will. Hence to argue that there is no God because things go wrong is self-contradictory. The argument affirms that things do in fact go wrong but denies the necessary conditions for the affirmation that things go wrong, that is, a plan for the way things are supposed to go.

Now let's shift our attention to the human experience of evil. As I have shown above, if there is no divine mind that can conceive and will the way things are supposed to go in the world, the concept of evil makes no sense in reference to the flow of cosmic events. Imagine, then, that we have evolved by chance in a universe in which there is no divine mind, no cosmic plan and no cosmic evil. Here we are. We exist for no reason and no purpose. For our coming into existence is a cosmic event and cosmic events do not happen for reasons or purposes. But as a matter of brute fact we exist as thinking, feeling and willing beings. And as thinking, feeling and willing beings we exist also as cosmic beings in the flow of cosmic change, of coming into existence and going out of existence, of the process of building up and tearing down that constitutes the universe. As cosmic beings we come into existence, exist for a while, then deteriorate and fall apart. Though there is no ideal plan for the way things are supposed to go, we can imagine one and wish it to be so. Though there is no divine plan for our lives we imagine our lives unfolding in an "ideal" way, that is, according to our desires. And we can perceive the contradiction between our ideal cosmic and individual plans and the actual flow of our lives in the cosmos.

As thinking, feeling and willing beings, we wish to be exempted from the cosmic processes of decay and death to which we are subject as cosmic beings. As a matter of brute fact we desire to live and experience happiness. We do not want to experience physical pain or emotional distress or spiritual suffering. When the actual flow of cosmic events contradicts our idea of the "way things are supposed to go" in our lives, we experience this contradiction and consequent distress as wrong, as misrelation and disharmony where harmony ought to exist. Hence on a human level evil is defined as whatever contradicts our ideal plan and thwarts our pursuit of happiness. And since this contradiction assails and destroys what we love, we hate it and rebel against it. At the human level evil is that to which we say "No!"

But this line of thinking rather undermines the argument from our experience of evil to atheism. We've seen that the idea of cosmic evil makes no sense apart from a divine mind that can plan and desire the way things are supposed to go in cosmic history. You cannot argue for the existence of real cosmic evil from the contradiction between the mere human desire for life and happiness and the way things actually happen, unless you assume the existence of a divine plan and a divine mind. And if there is no divine plan or divine mind, the "evil" human beings experience is not really cosmic in nature. It is subjective, relative to the brute fact of human desires and wishes. On the supposition of the non-existence of God or anything like God, at the cosmic level genocides, hellish wars, devastating tsunamis, catastrophic earthquakes, famines, cancer and all other hateful evils are not evil. Like the deterioration of a radioactive element or the death of a star in a supernova, they just are.

36

DOES THE PRESENCE OF EVIL PROVE THERE IS NO GOD?

In the preceding chapter I maintained that the argument from evil to atheism is deeply flawed and arguably incoherent. As long as one defines "evil" at minimum as "something that has gone wrong" we must also admit the existence of an ideal plan from which evil deviates. And "ideal" plans exist only in minds; therefore the argument presupposes the existence of minds, either a divine mind or finite minds such as ours. But robust atheism denies the existence of a divine mind, so atheism must also give up the idea of a cosmic plan for the way things should go. Apart from such a plan no event can count as deviating from the ideal for the way things should go. There is no cosmic evil and hence no argument from cosmic evil.

If atheists give up the argument from cosmic evil to robust atheism, perhaps they can construct an argument from the human experience of evil to robust atheism. Human beings experience some events in the world process as painful, horrifying and repulsive. Measured by human wishes, plans and ideals, events often go horribly wrong. How does the contradiction between human desires and judgments about how things should go in the world and the actual flow of events argue for robust atheism? Clearly the argument would have to be developed along these lines:

1. A divine mind would conceive and desire the same or nearly the same ideal for the way things go in the cosmic process as the ideal conceived and desired by human beings.

2. A divine mind would do everything within its power to attain this divine/human ideal.

3. A divine mind would possess enough power to insure at least a close approximation to this divine/human ideal is realized.

4. Things do not go according to this divine/human ideal; indeed they deviate from it dramatically.

5. Therefore no divine mind exists.

Obviously, the first premise is the crux of this argument. Since the argument is made from an atheist perspective, it cannot appeal to divine revelation to establish how the divine mind actually conceives and desires the world to go. It must assert that human ideals would be shared by any actually existing divine being. Apart from this premise the argument goes nowhere. But it seems highly questionable to assume that a map of the values, goals and thoughts of a divine mind that encompasses every event in the cosmos could be extrapolated from the limited experience of finite beings like us. Understandably, we place ourselves at the center of all things and think the entire world process should serve our private ends. But what evidence warrants the conclusion that a divine being must also place us at the center? Perhaps the divine being thinks and judges in ways very different from ours and views us as mere means to an end very different from ours. Indeed, there are many conceptions of a divine mind that are consistent with the human experience of pain, suffering and death. Maybe there are many divine beings that possess conflicting desires or perhaps the divine being is not omnipotent or its understanding of what is good differs dramatically from ours. Hence this five-step argument fails to establish robust atheism.

The failure of the argument just analyzed highlights something about atheist arguments from evil that is rarely noticed, much less explored: they do not argue from evil to "robust" atheism. I have never read an argument like the one I outlined above. I employed the unusual term "robust atheism" to designate the view that there is no God or anything like God, no pantheon of gods or divine mind, plan or law. In my view, the only atheism worth considering denies that mind or anything mental is a fundamental eternal reality. And this is what I mean by robust atheism. Modern atheism (from about 1770 to the present) argues from the fact of evil to the incoherence of *western theism* (a view of God influenced by Christianity, Judaism and Islam) and concludes to the nonexistence of the God of western theism. The Creator God of western theism is omnipotent, perfectly good and omniscient. Atheists argue that the factual existence of evil demonstrates that God cannot possess all three attributes. If God really were all-powerful, he could prevent all evil, if God were perfectly good he would want to prevent all evil and if God were omniscient he would know about every instance of evil. But evil exists; therefore the God of western theism does not exist. A variant of this argument contends that perhaps some instances of pain and suffering are consistent with God's existence, but there is so much evil in our world that no good end could ever justify it or make it right.

Clearly this argument does not warrant the conclusion of robust atheism that no God or anything like God exists. At most it points to the problem of reconciling a particular view of the divine cosmic mind (western theism) with the existence of evil. But this problem finds its natural home within a philosophical theology that affirms the existence of a divine mind. Only by a slight of hand can a debate about the nature of the divine and its relation to the flow of events evoked by the experience of evil be transformed into a debate about the very existence of anything like God. If you fall into robust atheism because of the argument from evil you have leapt far beyond the evidence. Some other motivating force must be at work.

37

EVIL IS NOT A THING!

The previous chapter concluded that however much our experience of evil might challenge belief in an omnipotent, perfectly good and omniscient God, it does not disprove or even challenge the existence of a divine reality as such. There are many views of the divine and its mode of interaction with the world that are perfectly consistent with the existence of evil. The importance of this insight can hardly be overstated, and I will explore its significance in a future chapters. For now we need to explore the nature of evil in a bit more detail.

Evil as Conflict

In a previous chapter I argued that describing an event as "evil" makes sense only if the event transgresses a cosmic plan for the way things are supposed to go. Evil is too strong and emotional a word to be used as a way to say "this is not what I wanted" or "I don't like this." In that chapter I argued that the concept of evil is evacuated of significance unless the thing we call evil is also "wrong." Hence the concept of evil entails the concept of wrong.

In this chapter I want to point out another quality of evil, not so much a moral quality (wrongness) as a physical quality. Whatever else one might say about evil, everyone can see that it involves disorder, disharmony or conflict. In a moral evil such as theft or murder the perpetrator abandons adherence to the moral law and enters into conflict with other people's interests or rights. Vices such as greed, envy and lust arise from inner disorder and generate outer conflict. Such diseases as cancer, heart failure and diabetes begin when the natural integrity and harmony of the body fails and degeneration sets in. I use the word "conflict" to stand for the family of physical qualities mapped by the terms disorder, disharmony, disintegration, antagonism, conflict and other like terms.

What is the origin of conflict? Conflict makes sense only where there is more than one thing. Why is there more than one thing? In the end, there are only two ways to think about the origin of our universe. Either it derives from one eternal reality or it derives from more than one eternal reality. In worldviews that teach that there is only one eternal reality—for example monotheism—evil cannot be eternal because evil becomes possible only when the one eternal reality produces the many things of the world. In worldviews that appeal to more than one eternal reality—for example polytheism—the possibility for evil is eternal because division itself is eternal. Many of the differences between the ways the world's religions and philosophies approach evil can be explained by which one of these two presuppositions they hold to be true.

In continuity with Judaism, Christianity teaches that there is only one eternal God who is the creator of the world and its diverse creatures. God freely created the world with all its diversity by his word. In the early centuries of the church, Christian theologians faced a challenge from religious philosophies that asserted the existence of two eternal realities, one good and the other evil. These philosophies taught that the existence and apparent power of evil can be explained only by the existence of an eternal evil power that stands in everlasting conflict with the good power. Otherwise, they argued, we would have to think of God as the origin of evil as well as good.

Evil is Not a Thing

In response to such philosophies Christian thinkers argued that evil is not an independent thing that can act on its own. Evil is disorder, misrelation or defective activity among real things. Evil is the condition of disorder itself, not a thing that instigates conflict against other things. And disorder is not an existing thing, like an atom, an animal or a human being. It can have no effect apart from the activity of things that exist. Real things can be ordered or disordered, but disorder cannot exist by itself. Augustine says, "I inquired what wickedness is; and I did not find a substance but a perversity of will twisted away from the highest substance, you O God, toward inferior things, rejecting its own inner life" *(Confessions* 7.16). Basil the Great also rejects the idea that evil is a real thing that can exist on its own:

> Do not consider God the cause for the existence of evil, nor imagine evil as having its own existence. For evil is the absence of good...For it is neither uncreated... nor is it created, for if all things are from God, how can evil be from good. For nothing that is vile comes from the beautiful, nor does evil come from virtue" *(God is Not the Author of Evil,* 8; quoted in Dumitru Staniloae, *Orthodox Dogmatic Theology,* vol. 2).

Basil's and Augustine's rejection of the eternal and independent reality of evil solved one problem but created another. If God is the sole eternal creator of this diverse world why is there disorder and conflict? The mere presence of diversity does not cause disharmony and conflict. Different things can be related harmoniously to achieve a greater whole. But how does a diverse world maintain its unity and harmony. No one thing within the world possesses the power to unify the whole world. If a brick were to impose its order on the house, it could at best transform the house into a brick. And that imposition would be an instance of violence and destruction. The Creator alone possesses the power, right and wisdom to unify the world of diverse things without doing violence to any of them. So, what disrupts the harmonious order? Two possibilities come to mind, chance or freedom.

Chance and Freedom as the Origins of Evil

Events that have their origin in chance or freedom are thought to break from the chain of events that preceded them and begin a new chain of events. Hence they can create order from disorder or destroy an existing order. Chance can be conceived in two ways. First, chance can be thought of as a spontaneous coming into being from nothing. Such an event has no origin and no explanation. It is absurd. Second, chance can be considered an event that occurs when two preexisting chains of events intersect in a way unpredictable from within either chain. A bird is flying overhead and I am taking my morning walk...I don't need to describe what happens next. There is no vantage point from which the first form of chance could be predicted, but for the second there is such a possibility. Someone outside these chains of events in a position to see both could predict the time and place of their intersection.

From an external point of view freedom looks much like chance. Events originating in freedom look somewhat spontaneous and they often disrupt the expected flow of surrounding events. Chance events often cause suffering, death and destruction and so can events originating in freedom. We see chance events from an external point of view but we experience freedom from within ourselves, as rational deliberation and choice. Hence we hold people responsible for their free decisions. We may curse chance, but we don't hold it responsible for what it causes. We attribute the suffering, death and destruction we experience at the hands of natural processes to chance. But most of the evil we experience at the hands of human beings we attribute to freedom.

But why doesn't God impose and maintain perfect harmony among the diverse things and free beings in the world? Why does God permit evil? Is the free will defense the best answer to the argument from evil? I will address these questions in the next chapter.

38

THE *REAL* PROBLEM OF EVIL

In the three previous chapters devoted to the challenge from evil, I claimed that the argument from evil to atheism fails rather dramatically and that what we call evil is disorder and conflict rather than an actual concrete thing or force. In this chapter I want to build on this foundation.

The two main contemporary forms of the argument from evil are the "logical argument" and the "evidential argument." The logical argument contends that the classical divine attributes of omnipotence, perfect goodness and omniscience are logically at odds with the proposition that evil exists. If God were omnipotent, God could prevent all evil. If God were perfectly good, God would want to prevent all evil. And if God were omniscient, God would know every instance of evil and how to prevent it. But evil exists. Therefore God is either omnipotent but not perfectly good or perfectly good but not omnipotent.

Such Christian philosophers as Alvin Plantinga have argued that the logical argument is not as logically unassailable as it seems to be. Even if God could prevent all evil, he could have a morally sufficient reason for allowing some evil. Suppose that a world containing free beings, even if those beings can do evil as well as good, is a greater good than a world without instances of evil but also without freedom. And suppose further that God cannot create this better world without allowing the possibility for evil to occur, since a creature's act cannot be both free and determined at the same time. Hence asserting the three classical attributes is not logically inconsistent with the admission that evil occurs.

The evidential argument from evil gives up the idea of a logical contradiction between the three classical attributes and the admission that evil occurs. Admitting that God might have a good reason for allowing *some* evil, the advocates of the evidential argument contend that there is *too much* horrendous evil in the world for any greater good to justify God for allowing it. In my view this argument is much harder to make or to refute. The reason is simple: it attempts to quantify how much evil could justify any possible good outcome. We have no perspective from which to make this judgment and no scale on which to weigh present evil against future good. The debate goes nowhere and turns quickly into an appeal to emotion and an attack on the character of the believer.

It is important to note that neither of these arguments (logical or evidential), even if you accept them, concludes to atheism. They merely point to an alleged contradiction or difficulty in the classical doctrine of God. And it should be obvious that our inability to articulate a perfectly coherent doctrine of God should not count as strong evidence for the nonexistence of God. Such a demand would be considered ridiculous in almost any other area of science or philosophy. If you have other compelling reasons for believing in God or affirming the classical doctrine of God, the challenge of the problem of evil need not defeat this belief even if you cannot resolve the difficulties completely.

For Christianity, the present tension created by sin, suffering and death cannot be resolved by rational arguments that attempt to balance accounts between good and evil. The resolution will be accomplished in the future resurrection and redemption of creation and is grasped in the present only by faith in God through Jesus Christ. The Bible gives no rigorous rational account of the origin of evil or why God allows it. Sin, suffering and death are roughly associated with freedom (Gen 3 and Rom 5:12-21), and sometimes suffering is said to produce good things in the long run (Rom 5:1-5; Heb 12:7-11; and James 1:2-4). But for the most part, New Testament authors take our existential situation for granted and focus on the salvation achieved by Jesus Christ in the cross and resurrection, they encourage living in the present in the faith, hope and love given by the Holy Spirit and they look to the future resurrection and judgment to correct all wrongs and make all things new.

For Christian theology, the most pressing problem of evil is not the disturbing question of why God allows suffering. It is existential fact that we are sinners, unable to clear our consciences or change our behavior, and that we are dying along with the whole creation. The cross is the ground and hope for forgiveness and deliverance from sin, and the resurrection is the ground and hope for death's defeat and life's eternal triumph. When the real problem of evil is finally dealt with the question of why God allowed suffering will be forgotten.

39

THE RHETORICAL ARGUMENT FROM EVIL

The most potent argument challenging belief is not an argument at all. The other two arguments from evil discussed in previous chapter attempt to maintain a logical form and a rational tone. Not this one! It rehearses in exquisite detail the horrors of war, the ravages of sicknesses and the savagery of human cruelty. It speaks of holocausts and genocides. It places the believer in a completely untenable position. The suffering described is so horrible, so unforgiveable that voicing any hope for redemption or for any good to come from it makes you sound like you are trivializing it.

This argument is sometimes called the "emotional" argument from evil, but I think it is best labeled the "rhetorical" argument from evil. I prefer this designation for the argument because it attempts not to persuade believers but to silence them with sarcasm or nauseating descriptions of suffering. It pictures those who believe in a kind Heavenly Father who takes care of us as fools blindly following an optimistic theory in face of its obvious refutation or as unsympathetic listeners unmoved by the most horrendous human suffering. In this setting believers are placed in the dilemma of either remaining silent and giving tacit assent to the argument or speaking and sounding foolish or cruel.

Voltaire's book *Candide* is the most famous example of using sarcasm to attack the belief that God allows everything to happen for a reason. The book tells the story of the misadventures of Candide and his companions as they witness and endure terrible wickedness and suffering. Dr. Pangloss is an optimist who believes that everything happens for the best. His constant refrain is that "this is the best of all possible worlds and everything happens for the best," which sounds absurd in the context of Voltaire's description of the death, dismemberment and suffering they encounter. What makes Pangloss seem foolish is not his deep faith that God will work all things for good but his silly presumption that he can see this with his own eyes and his tactless voicing of this opinion.

The most famous example of using agonizing and nauseating descriptions of wickedness and suffering against belief is the conversation between Ivan Karamazov and Alyosha his novice monk brother in Fyodor Dostoevsky's *The Brothers Karamazov.* Ivan explains to his younger brother why he rejects God's world and plans to kill himself when he turns 30 years of age: "Yet would you believe it, in the final result I don't accept this world of God's, and although I know it exists, I don't accept it at all. It's not that I don't accept God, you must understand, it's the world created by Him I don't and cannot accept" (p. 203, Norton Critical Edition)! Ivan tells story after story of innocent children tortured by heartless adults. But the most agonizing is the story of a little girl tortured by her own parents:

> These educated parents subjected this poor five-year-old girl to every possible torture. They beat, thrashed, kicked her, not knowing why themselves, turning her whole body into bruises; finally they reached the highest refinement: in the cold, in the frost, they shut her up all night in the outhouse, because she wouldn't ask to be taken out at night (as though a five-year-old child, sleeping its angelic sound sleep, could be taught to ask)—for that they smeared her whole face with her excrement and made her eat that excrement, and it was her mother, her mother who made her! And that

> mother could sleep at night, hearing the groans of that poor little child, locked up in that vile place! Can you understand that a little being, who still can't even comprehend what is being done to her, in that vile place, in the dark and cold, beats herself with her tiny little fist on her strained little chest and cries her bloody, unresentful, meek little tears to 'dear God' to protect her—can you understand that nonsense, my friend and my brother, my pious and humble novice, do you understand why this nonsense is necessary and created? Without it, they say, man could not have existed on earth, for he would not have known good and evil. Why should he know that diabolical good and evil, when it costs so much? The whole world of knowledge is not worth the little tears of that little child to 'dear God.'

Ivan concludes that no possible good that could be achieved is worth even one tear from that little girl. "I don't want harmony, for the love of humanity, I don't want it. I would rather remain with unavenged suffering. I'd rather remain with my unavenged suffering and unquenched indignation, *even if I am wrong*" (p. 212). Alyosha the believer is completely silenced. There is nothing to be said.

Ivan Karamazov is the literary expression of what came to be known in the mid-20th century in response to the Holocaust as "protest atheism." Protest atheism contends that any effort to find meaning in horrendous events of suffering diminishes that suffering and dampens our enthusiasm to fight against evil. The "unavenged suffering and unquenched indignation" must be kept alive for the victims' sake. Their suffering must not be made a means to a higher end.

As I said at the beginning of this chapter, the rhetorical argument from evil is not a logical and rational argument. Now I think we can see what it is. It expresses agonized rebellion against forgetting and minimizing the suffering of the victims of the evil that human beings do to each other. And it expresses an irrevocable commitment to keep alive the determination to fight against such evil. Christian believers can and should share these concerns. We must. *To believe that God will dry every tear does not mean that the tears were not cried or were cried in vain.* No. Hope in God does not exclude weeping for ourselves and others who suffer. Faith that God will make all things right does not mean that we are relieved of the duty to denounce evil and fight against it with all our might.

These thoughts are expanded greatly in the 25-page chapter ("The Rhetorical Argument From Evil") in my book, *The Faithful Creator: Affirming Creation and Providence in an Age of Anxiety* (InterVarsity Press, 2015).

40

CAN SCIENCE SHOW THERE IS NO GOD?

In the preceding five chapters I've dealt with objections to Christian belief that arise from the experience of evil. In this chapter I will begin to examine objections inspired by modern natural science. In general, people who object to belief based on science argue that science has discovered fully natural, lawful explanations for processes and phenomena that were in the past explained by the existence and activity of God. If belief in God is an inference from observed effect to unobserved cause, belief in God is no longer warranted. Since the beginning of the scientific revolution so many secrets of nature have been given natural explanations that there is no longer any reasonable expectation that we will find a place within nature for God to act. Even if natural science cannot *prove* there is no God, the argument continues, it has closed so many gaps in nature so tightly that belief in a God who created and is active in the world has been robbed of its explanatory power and, hence, of its rational basis.

Before Galileo and all the way back to Plato and before, the world was conceived as a combination of body and soul. In analogy to the human being, the world body was animated by a soul that enabled it to move. The distinction between dead matter and living soul was self-evident. Matter possesses no power to move itself or to cause change in something else. Only soul is active and causal. When people living before Galileo looked up into the sky they assumed that the movements they saw were the result of the rotation of all things around earth, which is the center of the universe. The Sun, Moon, planets and the stars moved around earth propelled by the world soul. It was a spiritual universe in which the activity of God and the spiritual world were obvious. Movement (the visible effect) was explained by soul (the invisible cause). And all of this was made doubly certain by our experience of our minds and souls in relation to our bodies and the external world.

Galileo and those that followed him argued that we should adopt a new analogy or model to help explain how the world works. Instead of the organic model of soul/body in which soul exercises its causality mysteriously by an internal organic connection, such as that we experience between our minds and our bodies, we should think of the world as a machine in which wholly material parts (ultimately atoms) interact with each other only externally. Movement is transferred from one body to another by external impact. In this way the mystery is removed from movement and change within the world, because mechanical interactions involve only relative spatial location, magnitude and direction and these can be comprehended by the clearest and most precise of all the sciences, mathematics.

Perhaps Galileo believed that there were spiritual and organic aspects to the world whose working cannot be explained by the mechanical analogy. But soon there were those who argued that everything and every process in the world can be explained exhaustively by mechanical principles, that is, by external relations comprehended in mathematical language. All movement in the physical world is cause by impacts of physical objects on each other. All phenomena are caused by atoms that come to be arranged spatially purely by natural means. Hence no inference from the beauty, intelligibility, fittingness, complexity and order of the world to a spiritual cause is warranted.

Much more could be said in response to this argument than I am going to say. Those who know something about contemporary physics know that the mechanical model is no longer held to mirror everything and every process in the physical world. It applies only to a narrow range of the world. The idea that the world is made of unbreakable atoms that relate only externally has been exploded. Other analogies and models now play a part: fields, waves, strings, etc. Causality is no longer central to scientific explanation and quantum discontinuity or indeterminacy has been added to continuity and determinacy. Many of the arguments against belief that were forged in the post-Galileo era no longer carry weight. Nevertheless the impression remains that somehow scientific explanations of physical processes exclude the activity of God.

In response to the arguments derived from the mechanical model, I want to remind you that what occurred in the early scientific revolution was a shift from the organic analogy to the mechanical one. But why should we prefer a mechanical analogy? Machines like a simple fulcrum and lever or even complex ones like the mechanical watch are easy to understand and can be put into simple spatial and quantitative terms. It would be nice if the whole universe were this simple! But machines are outside of us and we have no capacity to get inside them. Hence we assume they have no inside, no consciousness, no soul and no mind. Then we extend this analogy to the whole universe and conclude that the universe has no inside, no consciousness and no mind. But we do not know this! We have assumed it based on our external experience of simple objects.

My answer to the argument from natural science to unbelief or skepticism is as follows: The metaphors of machine, fields, waves and all the others derive from common sense observation of the external world. But there is one object in the world to which we have a most intimate relationship, not external but internal, that is, our own being, body, mind and soul. We experience within our very selves the power of causality and movement and freedom as our own acts. And that is something we can never experience in an external way! All physical science is but an extension of common sense experience of the external world. Hence science can never comprehend the spiritual dimension of the world. Only by taking our internal experience of ourselves as primitive and self-evident can we gain access to a spiritual dimension of the world. Why not take our most direct experience of reality as the deepest window into that we can experience only indirectly? I consider it completely absurd to allow external experience to negate internal experience! After all, both are human experience pictured only in the mind. In empirical experience we use without noticing the power of our minds to construct internal images of things outside the mind from sense impressions. But in the mind's experience of itself we experience the creative and constructive power of the mind directly. If we allow internal experience to have its say, the world will no longer appear as a meaningless machine or a mindless interplay of energy fields or a random world of quantum probabilities. It will appear as beautiful, meaningful, intelligible and spiritual. It would make perfect sense to view it as an expression of the mind of the Creator.

41

GOD IS NOT JUST A MATHEMATICIAN!

In the preceding chapter we explored the consequences of the early modern shift from the organic model of the world to the mechanical model. When we imagine the world and every process within it as working like a machine we place ourselves outside of everything and every process in world. Our point of view is always that of an external observer of how the surfaces of things relate to each other. The external viewpoint is maintained even if we modify the metaphor to include waves, fields and strings. And the interrelationships of particles, waves or fields can be described scientifically only in mathematical terms.

Now let's think a bit more about what science is and about what it can and cannot do. Afterward, we will apply what we learn to the question of Big Bang Cosmology and divine creation. As I pointed out above, mathematics is the native language of modern science. All other languages are at most pre-scientific. Yet as we will see, science cannot rid itself of all pre-scientific concepts. As a most conspicuous example take the concept of a "thing." Things are designated by names and properties. Its name designates a thing as a whole in its difference from other things: This thing is a dog, not a cat or a chair or a star. Its properties describe the distinct intelligible aspects that make the thing what it is and identify it as such. Cats meow, dogs bark and rivers flow. One of the properties of things is quantity. It seems to me that the only things that have but the single property of quantity are numbers. And I even have doubts about this, because it's difficult to grasp how a thing can possess only one property. Can the property be the thing? In general, the meaning of a thing cannot be fully described by expressing its quantity.

Pure mathematicians use only numbers and quantitative operations in their science. But as soon as you attempt to understand the empirical world in mathematical terms like physicists do you leave pure mathematics and begin to speak of *things*. And empirical *things* are more than numbers and can appear to us only through their non-quantitative qualities. The importance of this transition cannot be overstated, for it means that even physics, the most mathematical of all the sciences that study the real world, cannot escape the language of things and qualities into the clarity of pure mathematics. In order to increase our understanding of the world we experience through the senses physicists must tell us what *things* they are measuring. What is the mass of an *electron?* What is the electromagnetic charge of a *proton?* Physicists must relate their mathematical formulae to something we experience through the senses or their work illuminates nothing. And what is a proton or an electron or energy...or any of the other things physicists name? The answer cannot be a mere quantity! That would be a number. It must be a quantity of *something.* And things have qualities!

Physics and other natural sciences pride themselves on being empirical, that is, their goal is to explain theoretically the world we experience through our five senses. A scientific theory should be able to predict the occurrence of some event in the empirical world and the measure of success is whether or not its predictions turn out to be correct. Hence natural science begins with an empirical experience that needs explaining and ends with an empirical experience that confirms the proposed theoretical explanation. Between the beginning and end of the scientific process scientists abstract from these empirical experiences aspects that are amenable to theoretical generalization, ideally in mathematical language. But when scientists abstract only the quantitative information from empirical experience what do they lose? What is the status of this ignored information?

On the purely empirical level, before the operation of our minds in reading the sense data, we receive only physical impacts that cause physical and chemical changes in our sense organs. But unless we are completely skeptical about our ability to know the external world, we understand that raw sense data encode information that is decoded by the mind. The information communicated by the senses to the mind includes the quantitative properties of things, but it also includes the other properties as well. Galileo dismissed all properties other than the quantitative as secondary. He considered such qualities as color, heat and cold, and smell to be mental reconstructions of more primitive mechanical qualities and these reconstructions do not tell us the truth about the external world.

But Galileo's dismissal of qualities as secondary is blind to a huge fact: the sense data that the mind decodes and experiences as qualities *is itself information.* And information is created only by minds and is understood only by minds. Galileo and modern science in general are so focused on quantitative information that they relegate other types of information—esthetic and moral and religious—to the subjective realm. But why privilege quantitative information over qualitative information? If we read novels the way physicists read nature we would examine the quantitatively measurable properties of the paper and ink but completely miss the story. If however we read nature as we read novels we would find ourselves united with another Mind for an inside view of that Mind, its beauty, goodness and power. Why shouldn't the Creator use the physical properties of the world to impact the senses, which the created mind decodes into various qualities, which in turn makes meaningful esthetic, moral and religious experience possible?

42

CREATION OR BIG BANG?

The effectiveness of those contemporary objections to Christian belief that are derived from the discoveries of natural science depends on misunderstanding or distorting science's domain, scope and competence. In the last two chapters I've worked on clarifying these misunderstandings and distortions. Modern science attempts to explain data derived through the five senses by creating theories that predict future empirical states that, if they occur, support the explanatory theory. I realize this oversimplifies things a bit, because for different natural sciences—physics, chemistry, biology—the intermediate, theoretical languages differ.

Physics and chemistry are highly mathematical, whereas biology, while still mathematical, adds other types of relationships among the things it studies, specifically *function.* The category of function is needed in biology because this science deals with organisms, which are obviously organic wholes in which molecules, cells and organs contribute their part to the proper functioning of the organism. Hence biological explanation involves showing how each part functions in relation to the higher systems and finally to the total organism. However, in all natural sciences a transition from one state of the empirical world is related intelligently to a future (or past) state of that same empirical world by means of an explanatory theory that explains why the transition took place as it did.

In modern natural science, all the explanatory theories used to explain transitions from one empirical state to another appeal to the physical properties of the prior state to explain the change in form that is manifested in the subsequent state. There is nothing objectionable in this restriction. This's what empirical science does. But when thinkers claim that everything real and every event that occurs must be explained by the physical properties of the things involved, that the empirical method is the only way to truth and that all truth can be stated in empirical terms, they are grossly distorting science's domain, scope and competence. Given this false assumption about science, objections to Christian belief based on particular scientific discoveries (Big Bang, biological evolution) are redundant, for in their presuppositions the objectors have already ruled out the possibility divine action. But if you do not accept the assumption that everything real and active is physical and empirical, you need not accept the conclusion that the Big Bang and biological evolution compete with belief in God and God's all-pervasive action in the world.

The Big Bang

The Big Bang theory relates the present empirical state of the universe to earlier states and ultimately to the earliest state to which accepted physical laws apply (between 15 and 20 billion years ago). The theory accounts for certain empirical observations of the present universe. The universe appears to be expanding so that the further away a galaxy is, the faster it is moving away from us. The universe exhibits uniform (or near uniform) background radiation in every direction. These observations and many more are combined with the theory of relativity and quantum physics to conclude that at some finite time in the past the universe was so compact that everything in it was in one place (the singularity), that space and time had not yet emerged, and that the temperature was virtually infinite.

Let's not get hung up in a discussion of the Big Bang's scientific truth right now. Instead let's remind ourselves that even if its empirical claims are true, it cannot rightly claim to be the *whole* truth. The

Big Bang is not a theory of everything. It does not cover the same ground as the Christian doctrine of creation. It does not even speak the same language. It is a theoretical account of the development of the present cosmos from a previous state. It begins with an already existing universe, and it describes and accounts for the changes from earlier to later stages of the cosmos with theoretical articulations of the physical properties of the elements within the observable world. On a theoretical level it speaks the language of mathematics. That is the secret of its explanatory power but also of its poverty. It cannot speak or understand another language. There is absolutely nothing in the Big Bang theory that explains away or rules out the action of God in calling the universe into existence, giving it the form it has, guiding it to the place it is or leading it on to the destination God has in mind. The Big Bang cannot explain or rule out the reality of the qualities we experience or the mind we possess or the freedom we exercise. It cannot explain or rule out meaning, truth, beauty or moral law. It cannot tell you who you are or why you are here. If you have other grounds on which to believe in the reality of God, our minds, the intelligibility of nature, the moral law, human freedom and creativity and the meaning of cosmic history, the Big Bang theory of cosmological development poses no rational threat to any of those beliefs. It's simply a *non sequitur*, irrelevant, beside the point. As a cosmological theory, it is elegant. As an objection to Christian belief, it is lame.

43

DOES EVOLUTION OF THE SPECIES DEFEAT CHRISTIAN BELIEF?

Now let's consider the most popular "scientific" objection to Christianity. It is based on an inference from the theory of biological evolution. I am not a biologist, so I cannot and will not speak to the scientific soundness of contemporary theories of biological evolution. I am sure that my hesitation may provoke some readers to become suspicious of my motives or my "hidden" beliefs. But let me explain. In academic circles there are certain accepted marks of intellectual integrity and moral rectitude. I call them "politically correct confessions of faith." And even if you have no expertise in an area—perhaps you are even appallingly ignorant!—you are supposed to defend vociferously the accepted consensus of the experts and denounce equally vociferously non-conformists. Failure to do so may result in "excommunication." Many of those confessions of faith deal with topics of gender, race, class and sexual orientation. But they also include opinions about climate change, Big Bang cosmology, and biological evolution. If you say the wrong thing on these topics, you will be dismissed even by people who know nothing about science simply because you contradict the politically correct statement of faith. Hence I intend to speak only about what I know. I care very little for the politically correct creed. I care about the proper use of reason in seeking truth. And I know the difference between persuasion and coercion. And I know the difference between an ideology–a theory created to serve a pragmatic end–and a proposal motivated by a desire for truth and grounded in evidence.

Allow me to make another distinction. Objections to Christian belief that make use of evolutionary biology come in two distinct types. The first type objects to God's action in the world in a way similar to those who use Big Bang cosmology object. Opponents of this type argue that successfully accounting for a natural event by prior natural events makes divine action unnecessary. In other words, discovering the natural causes of events fully describes and accounts for them. It assumes that if God were to act in the world in creation and providence, God's action would have to replace natural causes and create gaps in the network of nature. As science fills those gaps, belief in God's action and even God's existence becomes less and less plausible. My response to this type of objection from evolutionary biology is exactly the same as my response to the Big Bang objections. Allow me to quote that response substituting the term "evolutionary biology" for the original term, "Big Bang."

"There is absolutely nothing in the theory of evolutionary biology that explains away or rules out the action of God in calling the universe into existence, giving it the form it has, guiding it to the place it is or leading it on to the destination God has in mind. The theory of evolutionary biology cannot explain or rule out the reality of the qualities we experience or the mind we possess or the freedom we exercise. It cannot explain or rule out meaning, truth, beauty or moral law. It cannot tell you who you are or why you are here. If you have other grounds on which to believe in the reality of God, our minds, the intelligibility of nature, the moral law, human freedom and creativity and the meaning of cosmic history, the theory of evolutionary biology poses no rational threat to any of those beliefs. It's simply a *non sequitur,* irrelevant, beside the point. As a biological theory, it is elegant. As an objection to Christian belief, it is lame."

A second type of objection to Christian belief inspired by evolutionary biology focuses not on God or God's action but on the Bible.

Some objectors to Christian belief realize that the argument from empirical science's explanations of natural events to atheism is less than convincing. At least they would like to employ additional arguments to make their case stronger. The Bible seems to describe the origin and development of the physical cosmos and of all the species of biological world in ways irreconcilable with modern cosmology and evolutionary biology. Much of traditional theology and many contemporary Christians take the creation narratives of Bible (Genesis 1-2) as divinely revealed history whose intention is at least partly to describe quite literally what happened at the beginning of creation. A person wishing to use the conclusions of evolutionary biology to undermine Christian belief would reason something like this:

"Christians base the truth of the Christian faith on the complete trustworthiness of the Bible. That is to say, they believe what the Bible teaches because it teaches it, and they believe they should believe what the Bible teaches because the church told them to do so. And they believe in the church because the Bible told them to do so–a vicious circle! The Bible teaches that the universe began a few thousand years ago and was created in one instant or in seven days. All the species of the biological world were created separately. But scientists now know that the present cosmos has existed for 15 to 20 billion years and has undergone vast evolutionary changes. We also know that life has existed on earth for many millions of years, that millions of species lived, thrived and are now extinct, and that human beings are relatively latecomers to the biological world. Hence, contrary to the assertions of Christians for hundreds of years, the Bible is not scientifically or historically accurate in cosmological or biological matters. And if what it says about science is not reliable, traditional claims for the authority of the Bible, and therefore for all Christian beliefs, fall to the ground."

As you can see, the objection from evolution turns on two issues: (1) does Genesis really intend to describe "quite literally what happened at the beginning of creation" and (2) is the entire Christian faith founded on belief in the authority of the Bible? Interestingly, some believers agree with atheists on issue (1), that is, the Bible teaches as literal history a view of origins incompatible with Big Bang cosmology and evolutionary biology. Additionally, because they think that acceptance of basic Christian beliefs must be based on prior acceptance of the authority of the Bible, they agree with atheists that if the adherents of these sciences are correct, the entire Christian faith is defeated. Given these agreements, these believers have only one way out. They are forced to deny the accepted science of Big Bang cosmology and evolutionary biology. But how can you achieve this if you have no expertise in physics or biology? Other Christian believers do not think that the first two chapters of Genesis were written to describe literally what happened at the beginning of creation. Instead, they were written as statements of faith in God as the Creator and Ruler of the world, constructed in dramatic form, which was the style of the day. Hence scientific objections to the biblical creation drama are completely misplaced.

As I said at the beginning of this chapter, I am not a biologist or a physicist. Is climate change real? Is contemporary evolutionary theory sound science? Is Big Bang cosmology sound science? These are questions for scientists to debate. I have devoted my life's energy to thinking about Christian faith and theology and about how we may make reasonable judgments about Christianity's truth and responsible decisions to take up the Christian way of life. In my view, the way into Christian faith from unbelief does not begin with accepting the authority of the Bible. It does not involve forming an opinion about evolution or the Big Bang or climate change! It begins with coming to believe that God exists and accepting the testimony of Paul, Peter and other original Christians to the resurrection of Jesus Christ. Only after these two reasonable judgments does the Bible have any claim to authority. Only then does the debate over the interpretation of Genesis 1 and 2 have any relevance. It is an intramural debate about how believers should best appropriate the message of these great texts.

44

IS CHRISTIANITY MORALLY OFFENSIVE?

I find it so interesting that many of the most strident opponents of Christianity attack it for its moral teachings. If you didn't know better, you'd expect these opponents to oppose the Christian moral vision with a coherent and profound moral philosophy based on an altogether different and better foundation. After all, to oppose and replace the religious and moral tradition that created the western world and shaped its moral intuition for over a thousand years is a pretty ambitious agenda. And since the objections I have in mind come from contemporary western people, you would think they would have given serious consideration to how they could escape the influence of the system they now criticize. Do you return to pre-Christian sources? Do you draw on non-western traditions? Do you attempt to derive a new morality from modern natural science? Only Friedrich Nietzsche and a few other adventuresome thinkers attempted to return to pre-Christian paganism. And most modern objections to Christian morality would apply doubly to pagan morality. Nietzsche criticized Christianity for its compassion for the weak, hardly politically correct today. Most non-western moral traditions are as conservative as or more so than the Christian tradition. And science can only describe the way things are. It cannot tell you how they should be. No, there is no alternative for modern progressives who think they have advanced beyond Christianity.

Self-conscious secularists, progressives and throngs of thoughtless people who echo them decry Christianity's prohibition of sexual activity outside of a marriage between one man and one woman. They reject Christianity's strictures on divorce and condemnation of suicide, abortion and homosexual activity. There have always been people who practice these things and who justify them in various ways. But lately we see a new hostility toward Christian moral teachings that views them, not just as backward and too demanding, but as evil. What accounts for this new hostility toward Christianity for its teaching on these subjects? The most obvious reason for the new aggression is political. The Christian moral vision dominated western society for many centuries. In the United States it has only recently become feasible for de-Christianized progressivism to turn the tables and become the dominant philosophy of culture. Christian churches and the Christian moral vision are what stand in the way of this transfer of power. Hence much contemporary criticism of Christianity can be explained by its political aims. But a deeper issue concerns me more than the struggle for political domination.

Why do secular progressives hate Christianity for its views of marriage, divorce, suicide, abortion and homosexual activity? I do not believe that it is simply because of what Christianity permits or forbids. In truth, it is Christianity's denial that individual human beings have the right to decide for themselves what is good and right. Christianity teaches that we do not own ourselves and that we must give an account to our Creator for what we do, how we use our lives and how we treat others. For de-Christianized progressives, Christianity's denial of their autonomy is deeply offensive. The only alternative they can imagine to individual autonomy is heteronomy, that is, self-alienating submission to the will of another individual or human institution. They cannot grasp the concept of theonomy, that is, submission to the will of God as the way to true human good. But instead of challenging the Christian moral vision with a coherent and profound moral philosophy, progressives appeal to the flattering but obviously false notion that individual human beings can be their own gods, determining good and evil for themselves. Perhaps Christianity's exposure of this fiction explains intensity of progressives' hatred.

45

THE SINS OF CHRISTIANS: EVIDENCE FOR CHRISTIANITY'S IMMORALITY?

In the previous chapter I argued that most moral objections to Christianity can be reduced to fundamental disagreements about the final authority for moral truth and the ends moral behavior should seek. The specific issues discussed by the culture at any particular time are merely occasions for the clash of contradictory fundamental perspectives. The view I called "de-Christianized progressivism" rejects all moral authority beyond the individual's sense of fittingness and any goal other than individual happiness as understood by the individual. In contrast, Christianity affirms the ultimate moral authority of the Creator, who is the absolute standard of right and good, and it views the goal of human action and relationships as the creature's correspondence in character and life to the Creator as revealed in Jesus Christ.

De-Christianized progressivism appeals to a different source of moral knowledge than that to which Christianity appeals. It cannot accept that individuals need moral guidance beyond their own experience and feeling. After all, if the goal of human life is to maintain a feeling of wellbeing and happiness in the present moment, who knows better than I when I am happy and what makes me happy? But Christianity mistrusts untrained and immediate human impulses. Human beings are sinners in need of forgiveness and spiritual transformation. It asserts that individuals' consciences need divine revelation, community discipline and tradition as sources of moral guidance.

If people holding opposite sides of these contradictory moral visions clash over issues such as those that excite our culture today without clarifying their deeper disagreements, they cannot possibly understand each other and will simply talk past each other. And since they cannot appeal to the same authority and do not seek the same goal, they cannot even reason with each other. Instead of asking why they cannot reason together about an issue and letting this question drive them to their deeper disagreements—and perhaps agreements on another level—they shift from reasoning to fighting. Opponents begin to view each other as irrational, insincere and evil. Words become weapons instead of vehicles for ideas. Carl von Clausewitz (1790-1831) observed in his book *On War*, "War is the continuation of politics by other means." Unhappily, von Clausewitz's aphorism describes only too well the current debate about morality. Christians as well as non- or post-Christians are often guilty of shifting too quickly from reasoning to fighting.

Many critics illegitimately confuse Christianity with the thought and behavior of churches and individuals who claim to be Christian. But it ought to be obvious that there is a conceptual difference between the essential teaching and moral vision of the original Christian faith and the practice of individual Christians and institutions that call themselves churches. Lay Christians and clergy have done and do bad things. Bishops acted like secular lords, amassing wealth and building magnificent palaces at the expense of the people while neglecting their duty to care for and teach the people. "Christian" princes conducted wars against other "Christian" princes. So-called "witches" and heretics were burned alive. Christian churches sought power in alliance with the political order. Clergy abused and still abuse their trusted positions by molesting children, living in luxury and seeking honor. Indeed, Christians and so-called "churches" do bad things, horrendous things, and they deserve to be exposed and denounced.

And it is precisely by the teaching and example of Jesus Christ and the original Christian faith that they are most decisively exposed and denounced! De-Christianized progressivism cannot possibly be as radical in its criticism. For it possesses no coherent principles by which to criticize such abuses. Non- or post-Christians also seek wealth, desire power and work to satisfy their lusts. And why not? They cannot appeal to moral law or divine judgment or the teaching and example of Jesus to redirect their lives toward the truly good and right. This life is all there is, and it is precarious and short. *Carpe diem!* Hence their criticism of the behavior of Christians and Christian institutions boils down to criticizing them for not living up to the teaching of Jesus and the original Christian faith, that is, it boils down to an accusation of hypocrisy. They don't raise any independent criticisms because they cannot. So, it cannot escape notice that an argument from hypocrisy to the falsehood of the ideals by which hypocrisy is exposed and denounced is self-contradictory. If the Christian moral vision is false, the charge of hypocrisy is evacuated of its moral force. How can hypocrisy be a moral failing if the system within which hypocrisy is condemned is itself false?

Surely it is obvious that failure to live up to an ideal does not disprove the ideal. Finding a bad Stoic does not prove that Stoicism is bad. Our experience of bad math students does not prove that mathematics is bad. Nor does describing the folly of bad Christians prove that Christianity is bad. Hence merely rehearsing the sins of Christians and so-called "Christian" institutions does not constitute a good argument against Christianity's moral vision. A good argument, that is, a rational argument, against Christianity's moral vision would, first, need fairly and accurately to describe that vision. Second, it would need to judge Christianity's moral vision defective according to an alternative moral vision, which as a system can claim as good or better grounding in moral truth. I do not accept expressions of emotion or sentences that begin with "I feel" or "everyone knows" or "we have discovered" or "history will show" as rational arguments.

I challenge the critics of the Christian moral vision to make an argument that meets these two requirements. Only then can we even have an argument. I predict I will be waiting a long time.

46

ABORTION, GENDER AND SAME-SEX UNIONS: HOW TO TALK ABOUT THEM AND HOW NOT

It is time to address some specific objections to the Christian moral vision. However, I do not plan to develop an extensive theological framework here. I did that in chapters 23-33 (Pages 82-126) of my book *The Thoughtful Christian Life: Essays on Living as a Christian in a Post-Christian Culture.*

"The whole world is under the control of the evil one" (1 John 5:19)

First, it is of utmost importance to distinguish between what is right and what is lawful. For Christianity, what is morally right is determined solely by God, the Creator and Lord of the world. Whatever contradicts the will of God is morally wrong even if the whole world should make it legal and declare it right. And whatever the Creator declares to be right will stand even if all nations condemn it. You may be nodding your head in agreement. Good. But we should not underestimate the persuasive and coercive power of law, its ability to confuse the mind and deaden the conscience. The legalization of abortion is a case is point. When the legal authorities solemnly pronounce a law to be in force or strike down a law previously held to be just we begin to doubt our previous judgment. And the cry of the people begins to sound like the voice of God.

To maintain a clear head in such situations we must keep the difference between the world and the kingdom of God clearly in mind. A nation's legislatures and courts sooner or later will make laws that reflect the moral condition of the people in that land. If the people are corrupt they will demand equally corrupt laws. And though the world is not completely evil—by God's grace there is a little light and a little good left—it is now, always been and always will be corrupt. This fact should not surprise us. Have we read 1 John lately?

> Do not love the world or anything in the world. If anyone loves the world, love for the Father is not in them. For everything in the world—the lust of the flesh, the lust of the eyes, and the pride of life—comes not from the Father but from the world. The world and its desires pass away, but whoever does the will of God lives forever (1 John 2:15-17).

> We know that we are children of God, and that the whole world is under the control of the evil one. We know also that the Son of God has come and has given us understanding, so that we may know him who is true. And we are in him who is true by being in his Son Jesus Christ. He is the true God and eternal life. Dear Children, keep yourselves from idols (1 John 5:19-20).

If we look at our world through John's eyes, we will not be so surprised or moved by the solemn pronouncements of human authorities that permit sin and condemn righteousness. "The whole world is under the control of the evil one." What do we expect?

Let God Judge the World

Allow me to make a related distinction. We are obligated to "obey God rather than human beings," as Peter declared boldly to the legislating authorities that were attempting to intimidate him (Acts 5:29). When it comes to a choice between obeying a human authority and obeying God, we must obey God and disobey human law. *But we are not obligated to force others to obey God.* There is a huge difference between a situation in which a human authority permits sin but does not obligate us to sin and a situation where a human authority mandates sin or makes it illegal to obey God. The authorities of the world have always permitted sin to one degree or another and often celebrated it. Understandably, Christians would like to live in a world where justice and holiness reign. And because we don't live in such a world, we may sometimes feel the way Peter describes the Old Testament character Lot as feeling: "a righteous man, who was distressed by the depraved conduct of the lawless–for that righteous man, living among them day after day, was tormented in his righteous soul by the lawless deeds he saw and heard" (2 Peter 2:7-8). Perhaps so, but we are not obligated as Christians to spend our energies in futile efforts to clean up the world's moral corruption. Paul gave some sage advice to the Corinthian church on this topic:

> I wrote to you in my letter not to associate with sexually immoral people—not at all meaning the people of this world who are immoral, or the greedy and swindlers, or idolaters. In that case you would have to leave this world. But now I am writing to you that you must not associate with anyone who claims to be a brother or sister but is sexually immoral or greedy, an idolater or slanderer, a drunkard or swindler. Do not even eat with such people. What business is it of mine to judge those outside the church? Are you not to judge those

inside? God will judge those outside. "Expel the wicked person from among you (1 Cor 5: 9-13).

When Arguments Are Counterproductive

The second point I wish to make may strike you as odd, but I think it contains a very important correction to the way Christians sometimes respond to external challenges to the Christian moral vision. We should take care to observe the following rule: *never try to prove something that is self-evident.* If someone denies that the tree in front of you really exists or that 1 + 1 = 2 or that you have a mind, don't argue with them. Don't attempt to give evidence for the obvious! Attempting to support something self-evident with evidence implies that the self-evident thing is not so self-evident after all. You will be making room for doubt where there was no room before you began arguing. You will be providing an excuse for people to act contrary to obvious truth. If someone denies the self-evident it is best to assume they are driven by an irrational commitment of some kind. We should respond with clear assertions, not with piles of evidence. Arguments and evidence move only those willing to be guided by reason.

Abortion

Do not be drawn into an argument about whether or not an unborn human baby is really a human being. The humanity of an unborn human being is an analytical truth. It is self-evident. Any evidence you could offer that an unborn child is a human being will only make that obvious truth less obvious. By entering the argument, you tacitly agree that evidence is needed and hence admit that the humanity of this little human being is not self-evident and that this truth is debatable. By obscuring the self-evident truth, you make plausible the notion that each individual has a right to make a judgment and a choice for themselves about the humanity of another human being. But this notion is false because the humanity of a human being is not an obscure and difficult question. It is self-evident. The only real question is whether or not we will honor the humanity of this human being. The only real choice people have is whether to do right or to do wrong. And if we want to critique the notion that abortion is morally permissible we can make no better argument that to assert tirelessly the self-evident truth and articulate a clear demand for a choice between right and wrong.

Gender

Do not be drawn into an argument about whether or not there are profound differences between male and female and what they are or whether or not these differences will be and must be manifested in the family, society and church. These facts are self-evident. It is as absurd to argue *for* the obvious as it is to argue *against* it. Members of families, societies and churches must converse continually on just how the obvious differences between the sexes should be reflected in the order and operation of these institutions. And particular arrangements must emerge from the conversation and not be dictated by an abstract theory, whether an abstract theory of equality or a natural law theory of fixed roles.

Same-Sex Unions

Do not be drawn into an argument about whether or not man was made for woman and woman for man. What argument could add to the self-evidence manifested in our very existence? Arguments that attempt to provide evidence that men are not meant to have sex with other men or women with women only obscure the obvious and create doubt. It is to admit that there is a real question when there is none. Additionally, in contemporary culture the subjective always trumps the objective. Presenting evidence—other than asserting what is self-evident—from the objective features of men and women for the conclusion that same-sex unions are morally wrong will always be dismissed by a culture that values subjective feelings above objective reality. Indeed for most of our contemporaries, the subjective is the truly real and deserves our utmost respect, but the objective, that is, the body and our material conditions, is merely plastic that we may shape according to our wishes and use according to our desires. Hence, as in the previous issues, the most reasonable argument is not really an argument at all but an assertion of what is self-evident, obvious and objectively factual over subjective obscurity and confusion. We have to insist that the only question to be decided is whether or not we will accept our created existence and thereby honor our Creator. The only choice is between right and wrong.

Why the Irrationality?

But if these things are self-evident why do some people argue as if they were not? And why do Christianity's critics accuse it of hatred for affirming things so self-evident? Let's address the second question first. Critics of Christian morality assume that each individual owns their own body and has the autonomous right to do as they please with that body. But Christianity denies this. Assessed from within the de-Christianized progressive framework, this denial looms as a threat of violence and oppression. It feels like an attack on human dignity and a mean-spirited effort to deprive people of happiness. Now the first question. How can people deny what is in fact self-evidently true? Because their moral philosophy of individual autonomy demands it, and they wish that philosophy to be true so much that it drives them to deny plain facts when those facts undermine their cherished wishes. Augustine of Hippo speaks about this human tendency in words that I must quote:

> "But why is it that "truth engenders hatred"? Why does your man who preaches what is true become to them an enemy (Gal 4:16) when they love the happy life which is simply joy grounded in truth? The answer must be this: their love for truth takes the form that they love something else and want this object of their love to be the truth; and because they do not which to be deceived, they do not wish to be persuaded that they are mistaken. And so they hate the truth for the sake of the object

which they love instead of the truth" *(Confessions* 10. 24; trans. Henry Chadwick, Oxford, 1991).

The Bible

No, I have not forgotten that the Bible's moral teaching on these subjects is clear, and for Christians the Bible's authority is decisive and persuasive. But people without faith can simply dismiss the Bible's commands, which apart from faith in Jesus Christ seem unreasonably strict and lacking in human compassion. In relating to outsider critics we can avail ourselves of the self-evidence of many moral principles and morally relevant facts, such as those I discussed above. Of course some people will even deny self-evident truths and manifest facts, but they cannot really evade the power of that self-evidence and facticity. In the end, reality wins! The conscience can be hardened but it cannot be erased. Hence a strategy of clear assertion rather than of self-obscuring argumentation holds the best promise of awakening deadened consciences.

47

"LIBERAL CHRISTIANITY"—NEITHER LIBERAL NOR CHRISTIAN!

So far in this book I have attempted to show that we can make a reasonable judgment to believe the Christian gospel and a responsible decision to take up the Christian way of life. Early in the study, in Chapter 3, I made it clear that by "Christianity" I meant the original faith attested in the New Testament. It is *that* faith I contend is true. And I responded to outsider critics in defense of this faith. But now I want to deal with those who "defend" Christianity by revising it to make it fit within modern thought and culture.

In the 17th and 18th Centuries many western intellectuals came to believe that Galileo's and Newton's scientific discoveries made it impossible to believe in divine revelation and miracles. God made the world and gave it its laws, and there is now no reason for God to interfere. God gave human beings the power of reason as a light to guide their way, and reason is sufficient for religion and ethics as well as for science and practical life. The first thinkers to adopt these ideas had little use for Christianity understood as tradition, church and worship. Religion could be reduced to living a moral life outside the church. These are the deists.

But in the early 19th Century something new came on the scene, liberal Christianity. Liberal Christianity accepts most aspects of the deist critique of orthodoxy. Along with Deism, Liberalism rejects miracles understood as supernatural events in which God reverses, interrupts or sidesteps natural law. Hence it rejects or reinterprets in a non-miraculous way the Old and New Testament miracle stories, including Jesus' nature miracles (resurrections, healings of leprosy, walking on water) and most significantly, Jesus' resurrection from the dead. Liberalism rejects the apocalyptic elements in Jesus' teaching and in the rest of the New Testament. And it rejects the substitutionary doctrine of the atonement. But unlike Deism, Liberal Christianity gives Jesus a central role as a religious and moral example and it retains a place for the church, clergy and worship in individual and social life.

During the 19th Century two major forms of Liberal Christianity developed. The first form emphasizes Jesus' religious experience and was pioneered by German theologian and preacher Friedrich Schleiermacher (1768-1834), who is universally acknowledged as "the father of modern theology." According to Schleiermacher, Jesus experienced a deep God-consciousness so intense that it overcame all resistance from the flesh. Jesus' God-consciousness differs from other people's experience in that he was able to inspire that consciousness in others. Only in this way is Jesus our redeemer and savior. The church is the community that cultivates this consciousness and passes it on to others. Christian doctrines derive, not from inspired words revealed by God and recorded in the Bible but from the feeling of absolute dependence on God that Jesus inspires. In Schleiermacher's now classic work on theology *The Christian Faith,* the Berlin theologian reinterprets every Christian dogma and doctrine in liberal way, that is, as reducible to the religious feeling of absolute dependence. For Schleiermacher, Christianity is not the religion *about* Jesus but the religion *of* Jesus.

In the late 19th and the early 20th Centuries, another liberal tradition became dominant. This tradition was begun by Albrecht Ritschl (1822-1889) and continued by Adolf von Harnack (1851-1930) and Wilhelm Herrmann (1846-1922). It focuses not on Jesus' religious experience but on his moral example. For Ritschl and his followers,

Christianity is based on Jesus' preaching about the kingdom of God, which calls on people to embody perfect righteousness on earth in a community. Jesus inspires us to believe that the cause of the kingdom will prevail over all resistance. Like Schleiermacher, Ritschl rejects miracles, the resurrection of Jesus, substitutionary atonement, the incarnation and other orthodox doctrines. Jesus is a human being who so identified himself with the purposes of God that he functions as the revelation of God in human form. He is not God in his being, but he reflects God in his character and actions. He "saves" by inspiring us to live according to the higher standard of love of God and neighbor.

The moralism that Liberal Christianity emphasizes is not personal holiness, that is, sexual purity, personal honesty and the absence of individual vices. It leaves this to the holiness churches and fundamentalist movements. The Liberal churches of the late 19th and early 20th centuries focused on bringing Jesus' message of the kingdom to bear on modern social problems: poverty, capitalism's exploitation of the working class, alcoholism, war and women's suffrage. Later Liberal churches continued this tradition, adding the campaign for civil rights for African Americans, women's liberation, environmental justice, gay rights and "marriage equality" for same-sex couples. In other words, Liberal Christianity follows and reflects the trajectory of what the consensus of the progressive element in culture takes for moral progress.

Now let's address the assertion contained in my title. Is Liberal "Christianity" Christian? Of course, it *claims* to be Christian, and it seems judgmental and rude to deny that claim. But surely it is not judgmental and rude to ask liberal Christians what they mean by the noun "Christianity" and the adjective "Christian"? What are the faith affirmations of Liberal Christianity and what are its denials? The Liberal Christianity I described above affirms Jesus as a paradigmatic religious man or a profound moral teacher and an extraordinary moral example. And orthodox Christianity also affirms these beliefs. But Liberal Christianity denies that Jesus was born of the

Virgin Mary, that he was the eternal Son of God incarnate, that he the performed miracles recorded in the Four Gospels, that he died as an atoning sacrifice for our sins and that he was raised bodily from the dead. It rejects large segments of the moral teaching of the New Testament because it conflicts with modern progressive culture. But these rejected doctrines and moral teachings were part of the original, apostolic Christianity. Many of them are confessed and taught in the New Testament as absolutely essential. It's obvious that in the New Testament era such "liberal" Christianity would have been rejected as unbelief or heresy and moral laxity. Does anyone doubt that had the Paul, John, Peter, James or any of the Apostles encountered someone teaching the liberal view of Jesus and morality that they would have denied it the name "Christian" and rejected it as "a different gospel–which is really no gospel at all" (Gal 1:6-7)? Call it what you will, "ecclesiastical deism" or "progressive religion" or something else. But if the original, apostolic faith is the norm for what qualifies as Christian and what does not, liberal Christianity is not Christianity at all but something else. But is apostolic Christianity really the norm for Christian teaching for all time? This is a decisive question. I affirm that it is, and I suppose liberal Christianity denies it.

My title also questioned Liberal Christianity's liberalism. How so? The word "liberal" is related to the words, liberty and liberate. Hence Liberal Christianity claims to be free and freeing. But from what is liberal Christianity free? From doctrinal orthodoxy, tradition and a strict and ridged moral code! How does it get free from those authorities? Does it assert anarchy or a latter day revelation? No. Liberal Christianity gets free from orthodoxy by selling itself to de-Christianized progressive culture. To stay relevant and on message it must jump on board with whatever progressive culture designates as the next area ripe for moral progress. Liberal Christianity has no place to stand to critique progressivism. It cannot appeal to tradition or the Bible or the divine authority of Jesus; it cannot even appeal to reason. It is always running to catch up with the next bold effort to liberate somebody from tradition and oppressive social institutions. And its

Christian baggage, as light as it is when compared to orthodoxy, slows it down so much that it is always behind the curve.

Liberal Christianity "defends" Christianity by giving up its most powerful and liberating teachings. It's an army that defends its homeland by surrendering the capitol, the best farmland and the most defensible heights. And in doing so it becomes powerless to challenge the world at the place where it most needs to be confronted, where it is most in rebellion to God. Like the ventriloquist's dummy, it has nothing of its own to say. It looks to its master for what to say next. And so I conclude that Liberal Christianity is neither Christian nor liberal. It's not even interesting.

48

WHY I FIND "LIBERAL CHRISTIANITY" SO BORING

I've been trying to put my finger on the essential difference between Liberal Christianity and traditional or orthodox Christian theology. In the previous chapter I mentioned several important differences. Liberal theology denies miracles, rejects the incarnation, reinterprets the atoning death of Jesus and accommodates to the ever-changing moral views of de-Christianized progressivism. These are real and significant differences, but is there one fundamental difference that unites these differences? Yes there is, and I think I've got it.

The apostolic faith and its faithful articulation in orthodoxy assert that in the existence and activity of Jesus Christ an ontologically real interaction between God and the world took place. By "ontologically real" I mean that God acts causally to change the *being* of world, to change the way it exists. In miracles, God actually works on the existence of the lame, the blind and the dead to change their real, physical being. In the resurrection of Jesus, God actually renewed the life of Jesus' dead body and brought Jesus to a new mode of existence. In the incarnation, God actually united the humanity of Jesus to Himself in a way different from all other human beings. The eternal Son of God, the Word, who was with God and was God, became flesh and lived among us (John 1:1-14). In the death and resurrection of Jesus, something actually happened between God and humanity that changed humanity's status from being condemned to death to being set free for life. God really counts and actually makes Jesus' sinless faithfulness ours.

In Liberal Christianity, real divine action, causality and change are missing. For Liberal theology, God works no change in the physical space/time world. Every action, every cause and every change in the world is exclusively human. The significance of legendary miracle stories is their metaphorical meanings. As parables, they teach moral lessons or illustrate God's benevolence or justice. All change occurs in the human subjective reaction to the story. They are not literally and historically true. Jesus' body was not transformed ontologically from death to life, from mortality to glory. No. The resurrection is a metaphor for the rightness of his cause. And the rightness of his cause is the really important thing, the essence of Christianity. How we know that his cause was right apart from the real bodily resurrection Liberalism leaves obscure, but the Liberal answer is obvious: we know it because of our own moral insight. Jesus Christ is not really the ontological union of God and man, as the orthodox doctrine of the Incarnation teaches. The incarnation is a metaphor for Jesus' complete devotion to God. He is united to God in love. And we too can be united to God in love. Jesus' death and resurrection was not really God acting causally to change the being of sinful humanity. No real change occurred. Jesus died "for us" only in the sense that he died serving a good cause that we also judge to be a good cause. His faithfulness unto death serves as an example of devotion to God and highlights the importance of his moral and religious cause. But his death is no more a divine act of atonement than the deaths of other martyrs. Its power for salvation is limited to the inspiration it provides for others to serve good causes.

Why this ontological shyness? Why such hesitancy to make assertions about real, effective divine action in the world? Two reasons come to mind. The first reason is a historical connection. Liberal theology traces its lineage back to the German philosopher Immanuel

Kant. In his epoch-making book *Critique of Pure Reason,* Kant argued that theoretical reason cannot reach beyond the world to speak about God. Reason's competence is limited to relationships within the world and it cannot speak about God's relationship to the world or the world's relationship to God. We cannot speak about God as the cause of the world or of any event within the world. For Kant, the only legitimate way to form an idea of God is through our own moral sense. God is a postulate, an hypothesis, required to make sense of our moral experience. Kant famously said that he had destroyed reason "to make room for faith." Proofs for God, miracles and all the other orthodox doctrines are vulnerable to rational critique and disproof. But the moral sense is immediately present and cannot be denied. It is a secure basis on which to ground faith in God and the moral life. Liberal theology exists because it accepts Kant's critique and it is afraid to let faith in God or the value of a religious and moral life depend on rational proofs or historical reports of miracles.

The second reason for its ontological shyness follows from the first. Liberal theology wants to insulate itself from rational critique of divine causal actions, such as those cherished by orthodoxy. It wants Christianity to be founded on a source of knowledge that is universally available and rationally unassailable. It does not relish having to defend the ontological aspects of apostolic and orthodox Christianity. Hence it downplays their importance. In reading Liberal Christian theologians you will hear a recurring theme, that is, the desire to rid Christianity of vulnerability to rational critique. According to Schleiermacher, the religious significance of Jesus' accomplishment does "not depend upon a visible resurrection or ascension, since of course Christ could have been raised to glory even without these intermediate steps: and so it is impossible to see in what relation both of these can stand to the redeeming efficacy of Christ...Hence we may safely credit everyone who is familiar with dogmatic statements with a recognition of the fact that the right impression of Christ can be, and has been, present in its fullness without a knowledge of these facts" *(The Christian Faith,* p. 418).

In dealing with the resurrection of Jesus, Harnack distinguishes between the "Easter message" and the "Easter faith." The Easter message focuses on the empty tomb and the resurrection appearances while the Easter faith "is the conviction that the crucified one gained a victory over death." Harnack is anxious to show that the Easter faith does not depend on the Easter message. He is not willing to allow faith in Jesus' message "to rest on a foundation unstable and always exposed to fresh doubts." We can believe that Jesus achieved the victory over death without believing that "deceased body of flesh and blood came to life again." According to Harnack, "Whatever may have happened at the grave and in the matter of the appearances, one thing is certain: This grave was the birthplace of the indestructible belief that death is vanquished, that there is a life eternal" *(The Essence of Christianity,* p. 162).

The late popularizer of Liberal Christianity in America, Marcus Borg (1942-2015), continues the theme begun by Schleiermacher. Borg explains his view: "Rather than focusing on "what happened," this approach [Borg's reinterpretation] focuses on the *meaning* of the resurrection of Jesus in the New Testament. What did it *mean* for his followers in the first century to say that God raised Jesus from the dead? Believe whatever you want about whether the tomb was really empty, whether you are convinced it was or uncertain or skeptical—what did Easter mean to his early followers? The answer to the question of meaning is clear. In the Gospels and the rest of the New Testament, the resurrection of Jesus has two primary meanings: "Jesus lives" and "Jesus is Lord."...Focusing on the empty tomb reduces the meaning of Easter to a specular event in the past. It makes the resurrection of Jesus vulnerable to skepticism...This alternative way of understanding Easter sees the Easter stories as parables—parables about Jesus. That is, it understands these stories metaphorically" *(Speaking Christian,* pp.111-112).

In these three examples of Liberal Christian theology you can see clearly their anxiety to remove any need to believe a miracle or to believe that God actually acted in history to change the being and existence of humanity and the world. Everything is about the "meaning," and references to God's actions are just metaphors. The "meaning" of miracle stories, which function like metaphors, is always something in humanity, a human possibility for morality or mystical experience. It never means God's action in the past, present or future. The Liberal "truth" of Christianity is always a "truth" that can be validated by experiences universally present in human beings. There is no real need for faith in the witness of Paul, Peter, James the Lord's brother and the others. No real need to submit ourselves to apostolic authority for instruction about what it means that God raised the crucified Jesus from the dead.

But why does Liberal Christianity want to make itself invulnerable to critique? Why does it wish to make it so easy to be a Christian? Here is my hypothesis. Schleiermacher, Ritschl, Harnack, and others realized that enlightenment rationalism and the progressive moral vision were going to marginalize Christianity and the institutional church in western culture. Christianity had been the dominant cultural force in the West for over a millennium. What a frightening prospect to envision living a post-Christian culture! The Liberal project centers on making sure that Christianity and the institutional church are not marginalized. For Liberal theology, the moral influence of Christianity is its most important contribution to western culture. It seemed essential to its survival. Hence to Liberals sacrificing the ontological doctrines seemed a reasonable price to pay to maintain Christianity's moral influence in a culture on the move. However, as I argued in the previous chapter, accommodation to de-Christianized progressive culture keeps Liberal Christianity on the run breathlessly trying to keep up. Eventually, it will have to give up the pretense of exerting any Christian influence on culture. Liberal Christianity has no prophetic message for progressive culture. And for this reason most people don't find it interesting or challenging or redemptive. The health of Liberal churches depends on receiving a continual flow of fallen fundamentalists and wavering evangelicals looking for a comfortable stopping place on the way to atheism and secularity.

Marcus Borg wanted to reconstruct Christianity so that it would not be "vulnerable to skepticism." I understand that desire. When I was a child the truth about God, Jesus and the Bible was as evident as the Oak trees and corn fields I could see from my bedroom window. As a child, I never questioned the faith of my parents and my church; I never even thought of questioning it. However when I learned more about the diversity of belief in the world and especially when I learned about atheism, skepticism, historical criticism, and other challenges to faith, my untroubled certainty was brought to a troubled end. I faced a choice. I longed nostalgically for the clarity, certainty and undisturbed confidence of childhood. Doesn't everyone? The soft voice of Liberal Christianity appeals to this desire. It promises to stop the progression toward complete atheism and nihilism. It offers, as you can see in Harnack and Borg, return to an untroubled faith invulnerable to skepticism and rational criticism. Just give up whatever cannot be validated by subjective experience and you will rest secure in the self-evident truth of Christianity! You can still attend church and celebrate Christmas and Easter. You can enjoy ceremony and sacrament. You can relish your enlightened superiority over fundamentalists. You can employ the Christian vocabulary of sin and salvation, justice and love, redemption and hope and the love of Jesus—all without taking any risks of being refuted by facts and rational arguments. As this series makes clear, I rejected this path. I came to see clearly that my childhood faith, the faith of my parents and the faith I was taught in Sunday School had a much better warrant as true Christianity than "invulnerable" Liberal Christianity. I realized that Liberalism's invulnerability was purchased at the price of its utter vacuity.

Indeed Borg is correct that asserting a real bodily resurrection makes Christianity vulnerable to falsification. The apostle Paul knew this. "If Christ has not been raised, your faith is futile…we are of all people most to be pitied" (1 Cor 15:17-19). But the bodily resurrection also grounds the claims of Christianity in objective reality, in an unambiguous act of God. In contrast, Borg's metaphorical understanding of the resurrection is grounded only in a subjective decision to connect Jesus to human aspirations. Hence Liberal theology is vulnerable to the charge of wishful thinking and making an arbitrary decision to attach subjective meaning to Jesus without a rational warrant. It is vulnerable to the critique that it possesses no real knowledge of God, that its claims about the kingdom of God, God's benevolence, justice and love are really human aspirations and characteristics projected onto an imaginary God. Liberal theology may look tempting to doubting evangelicals and fleeing fundamentalists. But it must look pathetic, nostalgic and sentimental to atheists and other post-Christians...and orthodox Christians.

In this book I have defended orthodox and apostolic Christianity. God really acted in Jesus Christ to conqueror sin and death. God really raised him from the dead and reconciled the world to himself through the suffering and death of Jesus. The tomb is indeed empty. "He is not here. He has risen!" The apostles are our teachers. I will not revise this message just to maintain power and influence in contemporary western culture. I am not interesting in making it easy for others or myself to believe in Jesus Christ and cheap to become his disciples. I am intensely interested in original, ontologically robust Christianity. Apostolic Christianity is as exciting as it is demanding, as deep as it is costly. Liberal Christianity is as boring as it is indulgent, as empty as it is cheap.

BIBLIOGRAPHY

Augustine. *The Confessions of Saint Augustine.* Translated by Henry Chadwick. New York: Oxford, 1991.

Borg, Marcus. *Speaking Christian: Why Christian Words Have Lost Their Power and How They Can Be Restored.* New York: HarperOne, 2011.

Dostoevsky, Fyodor. *The Brothers Karamazov: A Norton Critical Edition.* 2nd ed. Translated by Constance Garnett. Edited and revised by Susan McReynolds Oddo and Ralph E. Matlaw. New York: W. W. Norton, 2011.

Harnack, Adolf von. *What is Christianity?* Translated by Thomas Bailey Saunders. Philadelphia: Fortress Press, 1986.

Hartshorne, Charles. *The Divine Relativity.* New Haven: Yale University Press, 1948.

Highfield, Ron. *The Faithful Creator: Affirming Creation and Providence in an Age of Anxiety.* Downers Grove, IL: InterVarsity Press, 2015.

_______. *The Thoughtful Christian Life: Essays on Living as a Christian in a Post- Christian Culture.*2014

Kant, Immanuel. *Critique of Pure Reason.* Translated by Norman Kemp Smith. Blunt Press, 2008.

Marcel, Gabriel. *The Mystery of Being: Reflection and Mystery.* London: The Harvill Press, 1950.

Plantinga, Alvin. *Warranted Christian Belief.* New York: Oxford University Press, 2000.

Schleiermacher, Friedrich. *The Christian Faith.* Translated by D. M. Baillie and others. Edited by H. R. Mackintosh and J. S. Stewart. Philadelphia: Fortress Press, 1976.

Staniloae, Dumitru. *The Experience of God.* 2 vols. Translated and edited by Ioan Ionita and Robert Barringer. Brookline: Holy Cross Orthodox Press, 1994, 2000.

Voltaire, *Candide.* New York: Boni and Liveright, 1918.

Whitehead, Alfred North. *Process and Reality: An Essay in Cosmology.* New York: Macmillan, 1929.